OREO

By

Fred E. Bolden, Ph.D

© 2003 by Fred E. Bolden, Ph.D. All rights reserved.

No part of this book may be reproduced, stored in a retrieval system, or transmitted by any means, electronic, mechanical, photocopying, recording, or otherwise, without written permission from the author.

ISBN: 1-4107-0991-4 (e-book)
ISBN: 1-4107-0992-2 (Paperback)

Library of Congress Control Number: 2002096927

This book is printed on acid free paper.

Printed in the United States of America
Bloomington, IN

1stBooks - rev. 01/24/03

Table of Contents

INTRODUCTION V

CHAPTER 1 2

CHAPTER 2 19

CHAPTER 3 32

CHAPTER 4 48

CHAPTER 5 64

CHAPTER 6 73

CHAPTER 7 84

CHAPTER 8 95

CHAPTER 9 100

CHAPTER 10 116

CHAPTER 11 135

CHAPTER 12 163

CHAPTER 13 174

Introduction

As far back as can be remembered, I spent most of my boyhood and early adult life trying to be worthy, if that's the proper word, of being a part of a society that looked upon me and "my kind," a black American, colored or nigger, as we were known as in the Sovereign state of Texas, as not being a part of the American culture or even the human race.

Being born in the southwest portion of the country left little or no hope for a "colored boy" to realize any part of the great American dream, let alone allowing that dream to reach fruition. These almost intolerable conditions were a constant source of discomfort for a young boy with high ideals of achieving fame, fortune and recognition.

Oreo openly deals with the many social ills and cultural conflicts, which were commonplace, living in a white man's world and under his tyrannical rules. Oreo, shares the misery of oppression, the sorrow of disappointment and the mental anguish of suppression. During the early periods of growing up, there appeared to be an almost impenetrable wall of racial bigotry, hatred and total distain for anyone of color. This barrier stood like a soldier zealously guarding a way of life never to be breached by those they would consider unworthy or not a part of their race. Generation after generation stood at the gate of tyranny accepting and passing on the gauntlet to the next generation of their white brothers and sisters.

I basically placed my life on fast-forward in an effort to catch the brass ring before it was snatched away. I wanted desperately to move ahead into the future with the hope that life further down the road would be better for me, and all those like me. It was as if time never moved. I thought many times that God had forgotten my part of the world or had decided to write it off as not being worth his attention. I felt that my dreams, wishes and hopes were at a standstill and in order for them to take flight; I had to be a shaker and a mover. This caused me to grow up fast, perhaps faster than I should have.

My father realized that if the family were to have an opportunity to realize their share of the good life, he would have to move them from the State of Texas.

All except mother met the relocation to the Midwest with considerable glee. This was very evident when she first saw the family's temporary residence in Cleveland's slums. After a few short years of our arrival, I felt that I had reached a point in my life that I was mature enough to take on grownup responsibilities. I became a husband and father before I had completed being a boy. I substituted size for maturity, limited vision for certainty and above all, dreams for reality.

I lived long enough in the State of Texas to take on many negative traits that carried into my adult life. I became almost as bigoted against my own people as I had seen in the treatment of colored folks in the south. I did everything I could to separate himself from my own people. Throughout my life, the blacks that could be counted as friends could be numbered on one hand. I insulated my self, as best I could, from all that was black and as I grew into manhood and had a family of my own, I tried to insulate them from the black race and any part of the black culture.

I felt that the primary step to becoming a part of the main stream was education. I worked hard and ultimately achieved my academic goals, which gave me a measure of recognition in many parts of the country at various universities.

As a result of my second marriage, which was an interracial marriage, I had a multi-cultural family of predominantly white children. It was most important to me that I not unduly influence them, by virtue of my color, to marry into the black race. I never had blacks to visit my home and was all but hostile toward any black that attempted to date any of my daughters. I tacitly steered my mulatto son away from any black environment or relationships.

Although, I realized all of my dreams, the various routes I took toward the realization of those dreams were difficult paths. Over the years, my associations with people of color, in my capacities of a police officer, educator and employer, caused me to become more compassionate. My role as an educator brought me in contact with people of many cultures, which forced me to alter my way of thinking. In addition, as my daughters grew into mature women, they brought into the family a mixture of cultures, Hispanic as well as African American. I gave weight to the old adage that old habits and prejudices die- hard. It took many years for me to grow and bear fruits of tolerance for all mankind. Perhaps, my most significant period of growth was during my tenure of service at Wooster Business College, where I served as a professor and Dean of Student Affairs. In these roles, I found myself in a position of parent –in loco parentis (Parent in place of), for many of my students. I took on the plight of the under-privileged. Years later, I would speak of many of my former African-American students whom I would see, who thanked me for instilling in them racial pride purpose of life and dignity.

IN
MEMORY
OF
My loving wife

LEATRICE JOY BOLDEN
1938-1987

OREO

Standing left Fred Bolden Right Curtis Bolden, Jr.
Sitting left Irma Bolden holding Mary Elizabeth Center sitting
Curtis Bolden, Sr. Sitting right Delores Faye Bolden

Fred E. Bolden, Ph.D

CHAPTER 1

Is color a state of mind or a fact of genetics? God created man in his own image, according to the Holy Bible. His divine plan, after the fall of the Garden of Eden, was to have man reproduce and multiply, which guaranteed the continuation of the species.

God's plan was flawless. Unfortunately, man, as he has down through the ages, continuously tried to make God wrong. The Romans with their killing of Christians, Hitler, with his genocidal plan to destroy a total race of people and in our more recent history, the lynching of colored people in the south and some Northern states.

Like it or not, we are all still here. All mankind created by God, still exist and are reproducing.

This physiological process brought about my existence on planet earth.

I was born "colored," the then polite or accepted identification for people of black or other than white origin, which was the result of a union between two wonderful, God-fearing human beings.

Predicated on the fact, which should be undisputable, that God made us in his image, it naturally follows that my parents were homosapians.

On Sunday, December 27, 1931, a baby boy, the second of two was born to Curtis and Irma Bolden. 1931, was quite a year. The Empire State building formally opened, Al Capone was sentenced to 11 years for Income tax evasion, Thomas Edison passed away at age 84, U.S Unemployment reached over four million, Goodyear produced the first rigid Dirigible, Lionel Barrymore was awarded the best actor award, we were listening to such music as; "As time goes by and Love letters in the Sand." Max Schemeling was the heavy weight champion of the world, Razor blades were 4 for 25 cents, and the average income was $1,858.00 per year.

You could buy a car for $640.00 and a new house for $6,796.00. A loaf of bread was 8 cents, gasoline was 10 cents per gallon, a gallon of milk was 50 cents and Herbert Hoover was president.

I was in good company, like Willie Mays, who became a famous baseball player and Barbara Walters, who became a very famous Television personality, just to name a couple of famous people born that same year.

Fred E. Bolden, Ph.D

Fort Worth, Texas, was not unlike any other small town in the southwest. It had some industries but the main economy was based on cattle and oil. The colored population, as in all southern communities, lived in what was known as the colored section. I find it interesting that cattle were far more valuable to a white Texan than any bunch or an entire race of colored folks. We lived in the worst part of town; we were doled out the lowest type of jobs, rode in the back of the bus, and could not share the same sidewalk if a white person was on it. We were spat upon, beaten, lynched and our primary name was "nigger," with our primary purpose on this earth being to serve the needs and wishes of a white master.

I realize that you cannot help but wonder why I would have wanted to be like those tyrannical, cruel, insensitive, and bigoted "bastards."

My only defense is, it was not that I wanted so much to be like them, but I wanted what they appeared to enjoy. Looking at it through the eyes of a growing boy, it just looked like they had it all and I wanted my share. Perhaps, what I wanted most was the freedom and what I thought was my God-given right, to go as far as my abilities and drive could take me, without unnecessary man-made deterrents being placed in my path. Don't misunderstand me, I knew all great and not so great people, had to struggle to get to what they considered as having "made it," but I wanted the same breaks no more and certainly no less. If it was a decent school, a nice place to live or a place of entertainment, don't bar me at the door before giving me a chance. If it meant giving me a job that I was more qualified for than my white counterpart, then give me a shot at it. All I ever wanted was a level playing field. After all, God created me and I am an original and should be considered as an individual and not lumped with any mass. I knew this even as a boy.

My childhood began much like other Black-Americans, born during the depression years in any southern town in USA. Despite the cultural and economic conditions under which we lived, I felt that my family had it pretty good. My family consisted of Reverend Curtis Bolden (Daddy), Irma Kathleen (Mother), or as daddy called her "Kate," Curtis Junior, Delores Faye and Mary Elizabeth.

Daddy was the basic center of the family's world. He was, what was then known as, a "jack-leg preacher," which meant he preached in the church but had to keep a job to support the family. Colored churches were, for the most part poor, like it's members. Having it pretty good is not to suggest that daddy made the playing field level.

It meant he kept his family well fed, clothed and housed, which, as one looks back, was no easy task. Mother kept busy the entire day tending the needs of our family.

Daddy worked long hours at a boarding house by the name of" Simpson's Boarding House," so named after it's owners, Jenny and Buck Simpson. Mrs. Simpson was known as and called Aunt Jenny and gave all the appearances of being a kindly old lady.

In this case "old" meant around 40-50 years old. Aunt Jenny and Mr. Buck were divorced. As such, he was seldom ever seen but, from what can be remembered, he gave the appearance of being a typical southern "redneck."

Simpson's had a jewel in daddy Bolden, he was young, strong and did everything from repairing broken windows, cleaning, shopping and tending to the Simpson family's needs on command. I can remember how he responded to Mrs. Simpson when she would give him an order. "Yes mum I'll take care of it." She knew, that when daddy said he would take care of it, it would be done.

Mrs. Simpson would tell Curt Junior and I, when we worked there after school that "Your father is just like one of the family." I didn't know it then, that their dog was also like one of the family. No matter how she spoke of daddy, they never let him forget that he was still a "nigger" and was no different than any other one.

Although racial bigotry was a part of life, no, not a part of life, in Texas, it was the way of life, daddy tried to shield his family from the mental anguish of being a part of a society that considered his family as being less than human an on a par with chattel.

Mother worked full-time also. She was a mother, housekeeper and wife. Although, many colored housewives worked outside of the home, daddy felt that mother had more than enough to keep her busy raising us. Mother never held a job outside of our home.

One of my most cherished memories of this period was when daddy would come home from work, Curtis Junior and I would be waiting for him at the door. He would be weighted down with bags and pans in both arms filled with food that had been left over from the boarding house kitchen. Curt and I aimed for one of daddy's legs and promptly positioned our bottoms on one of his feet and hitched a ride into the kitchen. I can still hear mother telling us to let daddy get in the door and "get off from your daddy, he's tired."

If I close my eyes and concentrate, I can smell those rolls, breaded steaks, potatoes and gravy. From that small part of the big picture, our family was truly blessed.

We never saw a hungry day. During those years, there were so many people without food or a decent place to stay. Nothing came easy for daddy. If one had to describe our father in just two words they would be "hard worker." It was so evident in small ways. Such as, no matter where the family lived, he always left that place better than when we lived in it. Daddy provided for the family's every need, just as does Jesus Christ for the believer. No matter how tired he was he would find time to repair or change or paint. I remember in one place that we had lived; he had to put in a complete floor from the ground up.

Other than going to church, mother's pleasures were simple. She would listen to the soap operas on the radio while folding clothing and eating "Argo starch," which came in pieces that were solid, which she thoroughly enjoyed. Once in a while, she would allow us kids to have a lump or two. You know, it tasted pretty good.

I vividly remember one of the places we had lived, it was on a street called Bluff Street, which was a combination colored and Mexican neighborhood. Bluff Street was a long steep hilly street covered with gravel and bottomed out at some woods and a riverbank. I used to run down Bluff Street and being a very clumsy kid, I kept my share of skinned knees and bruised elbows. There was only Curt and I, when we lived there.

Neither Delores Faye nor Mary Elizabeth had been born yet, but Faye was on the way. One would question how we did it but our entire family lived in two rooms and shared a kitchen and bathroom with other tenants. During the family's stay on Bluff Street, I came down with Pneumonia. There were no antibiotics during those days. As such, I had to be treated at a hospital.

I was taken to Dr. Ransom's Hospital, the only hospital where colored were admitted. It was a hospital reasonably typical of the times. Although, as a colored boy, I never saw a white hospital.

Dr. Ransom's Hospital, the name of the only colored medical facility, had wooden floors and white iron beds. The food was good and the nurses were dressed up in the whitest uniforms I had ever seen. They treated me like a little king.

I had great fun with them. After a few days in the hospital. Mother and daddy came and took me back to our two-room part of a house. For the next few days, I was given one of the rooms all to myself.

Mother and daddy were told to keep me in a cool room and what foods to feed me.

I enjoyed the special attention mother and daddy gave me during my illness.

As my health returned, so did school. School, in this case meant a one-room schoolhouse built on stilts at the bottom of the Bluff Street hill. In as much as the location of the school was in the colored section, our two-room part of a house was just a short distance from the school. There was a certain quaintness about this old building. It had been painted an awful yellow and had no frills. This old wooden framed room was nestled amidst a forest filled with tall pecan trees with the River as a backdrop. Each student was assigned a desk/seat unit; you know the one with the letup desktop and an inkwell. In the same room was a section of a wall with hooks attached to hang our coats. The floors were made of wood and creaked when you walked over them and the room smelled like school, if one can associate a smell with such a facility. This entire academic splendor was reined over by a stern but pleasant teacher, who taught three grades in the same room. She had all the skills required to dispatch education and extended motherhood. I was never a brilliant student; I depended on an affable personality and good behavior, which worked well with my teachers. However, it was not so with mother. Unlike me, Curt made every effort to do his very best and get the best grades he possibly could. As for me, all I wanted to do was to read funny books (comics) and play. Mother's concern about me not having homework was brought to a head when mother decided that she would make an unannounced visit to my school. On the day she arrived, She wore a freshly- ironed Print dress complete with white gloves and a white hat. As mother entered the room, Mrs. Green, my teacher, cordially greeted her. After their exchange of greetings, they left the room. It seemed like they were out for a long time. When Mrs. Green finally returned, she smiled at me and continued with our lesson. I was most anxious to get home that day. I made no stops. There was no picking up rocks to throw or the kicking of an old tin can. I walked directly home. Mother had changed from her nice dress and was busy preparing the evening meal. Without hesitation, she shared with me the topic of her conversation with Mrs. Green. It was about me, of course.

Mrs. Green had told her that I was one of her smartest students and she had no reason to worry about my homework as most of the time, I did it while in school so that I could devote more time to playing. I was richly rewarded with many hugs and kisses, which I thoroughly enjoyed, from mother. It wasn't long after I got out of the hospital that we moved. The house that we moved into, was to me, the biggest house I had ever seen. It was made of wood and had been recently painted white and was located right next door to a church and for good reason, it was the church parsonage of Rosedale Avenue Church of God In Christ, so named because of its location on Rosedale Avenue. I was most struck by this house. It had an enormous back yard and a large garage, for which we had no car and plenty of room to play. As I continued my initial survey of our new home, I made a visual but cursory look at the surrounding area. The one thing that was very noticeable was the absence of a nearby school. Now I know many of you reading this book will be able to relate to some of the old wives' tales about how far our parents and grandparents had to walk to school. You know, the one about having walked 25 miles each way on a dirt road with no shoes on their feet or some other story about their hard times when they were going to school. Well…I'm going to give you another one. My new school wasn't 25 miles away but it sure was a far piece from home. I remember we had to walk for what appeared to be miles and miles up Rosedale and when we reached the end, there they were, a whole bunch of wooden buildings that looked nothing like the one building that I had been used too. Rosedale Avenue was a very wide and busy street.

Most of the houses looked like the house next to it and of course, colored folks lived in all of them. There was another drawback with our new home; every time the church doors opened, we had to be there. If not first in line, shortly thereafter. Every time an out of town preacher came to town, we had to make room for him to sleep in our house. The big day around our home was Sunday. The activity in the house was raised to a near level of pandemonium with mother and daddy cooking, getting dressed, doing last minute pressing and getting each of us kids getting ready. Whenever we had a guest in the house, the food bill of fare would do a southern mansion justice. It was not uncommon for us to have oatmeal, bacon, potatoes, and sausage, hot biscuits in addition to such delicacies as fried chicken, brains and eggs and grits. All of this took place before Sunday school.

Going to church was a major part of our family life. I still marvel to this day at how mother managed to do all she had to do on Sunday morning. I can see her now stirring some grits or rice in a pot on the stove, holding Faye on one hip while ironing out a wrinkle from her dress and once in a while, yelling at me to stop playing and get ready.

Daddy was right there helping with whatever he could in order to get us to the church on time. Sunday church was an all day affair. It started with Sunday school, with a break for lunch or dinner and then we returned for the rest of the evening. It was not uncommon for a single sermon to take several hours or I thought it was several hours. In reflection, now that I'm a Christian, I don't think I have ever seen a body of believers, like those old saints. They sang, danced, sang, danced and then they sang and danced some more. I say danced but during those times it was known as "shouting." There was such rejoicing that one would think that there were no problems in the world. The preacher would scream out a few words which were followed by a number of Amen responses from the congregation, followed by a few more words and a lot of amen's. It was not uncommon; when the Holy Spirit hit that the entire church would break out shouting during the sermon. When the sermon finally ended, an altar call was made (an invitation to accept Christ as your Savior). This meant coming down front where there was a series of wooden benches and kneeling down on them for prayer. Behind each kneeling person was an already saved person giving the kneeler instructions, which were simple enough. All you had to do was just keep calling on the name of Jesus. They would tell you to just keep saying Jesus, Jesus, and Jesus. People at the altar would be crying, slobbering at the mouth and screaming out the name of Jesus. The candidate for salvation had to speak in tongues (speak another tongue known only to God, based on the book of Acts chapter 13 verse 6 of the Holy Bible), their interpretation of which might not have been entirely accurate. Although, I now recognize and most certainly appreciate the value of my early church life, I found little or no joy in going to church, sitting on those hard wooden benches and listening to some long winded preacher hollering for several hours about something that I did not understand. This was not my idea of fun. I didn't understand it then but the church was all most colored people had. They had no future except in their strong belief in Jesus Christ.

Guess what? They were right. Living the Christian life in the church meant that you reframed form smoking, the drinking of strong drink, wearing make up, and going to picture shows. During certain holidays, we would have church picnics and that was always a lot of fun. There were enormous amounts of food to eat and many games for us kids to play. My favorite was cranking the handle on the manual ice-cream maker. Except for going to church all the time, life was pretty good for me and the rest of the family. We had plenty of food, a nice house and lots of room to play. In fact, there were many times when we had so much food, that mother was able to feed bums that came to the door for hand-outs. It made no difference to her if they were black or white; she treated them all the same. People gave us clothing from daddy's work and little by little I made new friends. How blessed we were to have a caring mother and a father who lived for God and their family. There were many who were not so blessed.

Most of the neighborhoods where colored people were forced to live were dotted with old run down houses, stripped out automobiles old discarded washing machines and you name it. Daddy and mother would not allow us to live like that. Mother kept us clean and healthy. The clean part, as it applied to me, was a fulltime job all by itself.

Mother would send me to school all neat and clean and upon my return, my shirttail would be hanging out and soiled. On one occasion, there was a reason for my appearance. There was a fellow band member, in the boy's band that Curt and I were members of, who enjoyed jumping on me whenever our band went out of town to play. One day, while returning from school, William Gilliam, his name, along with some of his friends, were walking down Rosedale, while my friends and me were walking down the other side.

My friends started to egg me on to fight William. After much urging, I became sort of brave and invited William over to my side of the street. He took me up on my invitation. When he arrived, we immediately got into it. It was mostly loud talk, shoving, snorting and pulling of clothing. However, when the dust settled and the snot stopped running, I was declared the winner. Now came the going home. Suddenly, my mother's warnings about not fighting were in my thoughts. I rationalized further. Hey! I'm the victor. I know she'll understand, just this once. Somehow, that didn't mean much at this point in time. Here I was with my shirt almost torn off, trousers ripped and more dirt on me than was on the ground. Upon my arrival, mother was home, as usual. She quickly noticed that I was a lot more disheveled than I was normally. She inquired as to what had happened.

I told her the story and she promptly gave me a lecture on the evils of fighting with a stern warning never to fight again. William Gilliam and I became good friends, after I beat his butt. For the next few days, I walked with my head a little bit higher in the air. MY best buddy, at the time, was a boy named Larry Bass, who played a terrific Trumpet and one other boy, whose name I cannot remember and Roscoe Jones. The three of us made up our "gang." Gang did not mean what it means in today's society. Gangs, during those times, meant that you and the guys ran around together for the sole purpose of having clean and wholesome fun. Our gang was called "The Thunder Clouds." Our logo was a cloud with a thunderbolt going through it. Our favorite pastime was walking through the woods looking bad to each other.

Chapter 2

Secured in my manhood, at around the ripe old age of 10, as if guided by instinct, I had my very first sexual encounter, if you could have called it that. I discovered the joy and excitement of masturbating. I don't know what triggered this activity. I know the textbook reasoning now, however, what does a little boy know about that kind of stuff. The only thing I knew was that it felt good.

I was very precocious for my age and felt that I had a handle on it (no pun intended).

After several engagements of hand and body, I diligently indulged myself on an almost daily basis. I allowed my fantasies to mentally roam the female population and summon them to do my sexual bidding.

I remember on one occasion, I became so enthralled, during my act of self-gratification that I injured the object of my affection, causing blood to issue from its integument covering.

In as much as I couldn't go to mother or daddy with this problem, I administered first aid on myself. After carefully diagnosing my situation, I considered it to be not serious and promptly applied generous amounts of Iodine and alcohol. Boy! Did that ever hurt. For the next few days, all sexual activity was suspended.

The seasons changed and the approach of our first Christmas on Rosedale Avenue was at hand.

Although, times were hard and money was tight, as children we still had our dreams and wishes for Christmas, which we openly shared with mother and daddy. As Christmas drew nearer and nearer, I grew more anxious.

I remember the night just before our first Christmas on Rosedale. I was so excited that I just knew I would never go to sleep, but sleep did come and the night passed. It was Christmas morning 1939 when a glimmer of light seeped through our bedroom window causing my eyelids to open like they had springs in them. I leaped out of bed and quickly ran into the living room, where mother and daddy had placed a large beautifully decorated pine tree. You must understand, that during those times, the living room was the best-kept room in the house. As such, it was a place of honor for our tree.

Every couch and chair was covered with tightly fitted plastic and each table was adorned with a lovely lace cloth. It was an accepted fact that the living room was not for living in but for company only.

As I approached the doorway to the living room, that place of hallowed sanctity, normally out of bounds for us kids, I spied two big two-wheeled bicycles. I let out a scream so loud that anyone in the house that was not awake would surely be awake after my bellowing.

I ran quickly to one of the waiting green and silver chariots and mounted it with the expertise of a seasoned rider. It made no difference to me that it was a used bike and one of the wheels rubbed against the frame. To me, it was brand new.

I could never have loved mother and daddy more than at that very moment. Curtis was excited but managed to be a bit more reserved.

I raised the kickstand and headed for the center of the living room but before I had barely started to roll, I was stopped by mother and warned that I could not ride my bike in the house.

I dressed myself as quickly as I could, postponed the teeth brushing and face washing and returned to pick up my Green Hornet's mobile (a famous radio series during those times known as The Green

Fred E. Bolden, Ph.D

Hornet and Cato). I carefully wheeled it around the furniture out the front door and onto the sidewalk.

Christmas day was cold but there was no snow. Mother yelled out a warning to me not to go into the streets with my bike and make sure that my coat was buttoned up. I rode up and down the sidewalk at the speed of lightning. I was like a racing bullet. The noise from the rubbing tire against the frame became my engine and I would take off in the clouds or some distant place at any minute.

Christmas, 1939 passed, as did the winter months. Rosedale Avenue was pretty much void of trees except for several Chinaberry trees in our back yard, which held a reserve of switches used by mother to administer corporal punishment when required.

I want to tell you, those Chinaberry switches could really sting you. Springtime was great. It signaled the end of school and more outside playtime. I enjoyed listening to the radio when we couldn't go outside to play.

I remember as the day would draw to a close, I can still see mother setting in her rocking chair listening to her favorite soap opera and munching on lump after lump of Agro starch. On Friday nights, we were allowed to stay up and listen to The Inner Sanctum, with it's creaking door. That was one scary program. With the lights out and only that small yellow light from the radio dial in the room, it was even scarier. During the day, after school, we could listen to Buck Rogers, The Green Hornet and Cato and the all time favorite, The Lone Ranger. The two radio events that held the attention of the entire family was whenever President Roosevelt spoke and when Joe Louis fought. Life was simple and a lot of fun for us kids. Drugs and gang violence was unheard of. Alcohol or tobacco was never used or allowed in our home.

I remember when a few of us fellows got together and cut a few branches from a grape bush and struck a match to it. We called that smoking. It was so bitter that I never tried smoking again.

The few young boys, who did smoke, had to roll there own, just, as did most smokers who could not afford commercially rolled cigarettes.

Spring and summer brought about another major event in the Bolden Household. It meant a time of travel. We would prepare for that long ride from Fort Worth to Dallas, which was 31 miles. To us kids, that was a big deal.

Although, we didn't own a car, daddy would borrow one of Mrs. Simpson's cars, the owner of the establishment where daddy worked, and pile us in it and down the Dallas Pike we would go. Because it was such a long trip, we could only go once each year. Mother packed sandwiches for the ride and jugs of lemonade.

What a joy it was to get a chance to visit Mama, mother's mother, whose name was Savannah, my Aunts and all my cousins.

The high point of our Dallas trip for me was getting to be with my cousin, Alfred. Alfred was older than I but we had a lot in common. We both liked to look at the girls. He took me around all of his friends and we spent hours talking about everything.

Unfortunately, I had very little to contribute except what I made up in my imagination.

After all, I wasn't about to tell by cousin that the only sexual experience I had were imaginary and ended up in sessions of ardent masturbation.

Besides seeing my cousin, Alfred, I wanted to fill my belly with Mama's Sugar cookies.

To this day, I have never tasted a sugar cookie like Mama's. There was no one like Mama. She was soft-spoken, easygoing and mild mannered.

I can still see her in her back yard standing over a large black kettle atop a roaring fire. During those days, most colored folks made their own soap by mixing lye and grease that had been saved from cooking fat. The process required that the mixture be boiled. During the boiling process, it had to be constantly stirred. I would beg Mama to let me stir. After a lot of begging, she looked down at me and with a warm but stern face and a gentle voice she said to me, "Ba-brother, my knick name, don't you get to close to that fire." After the mixture had cooked to the proper consistency, it was allowed to cool and then, it was cut into blocks, which were larger than the regular soap bars.

Each time we visited Dallas; the pace was fast moving and filled with activity. In as much as all of mother's family lived in the Dallas area, we had lots of visiting to do in a short period of time. All of the family lived in Dallas, except my Uncle Fred, after whom I was named. Uncle Fred lived out from Dallas and owned a small truck farm on which he raised hogs and a few vegetables. Uncle Fred would drive into town and pick us up in his old Ford pickup truck and cart us off to his farm. Riding in the back of that old truck was so much fun.

On this particular trip, while on the way to Uncle Fred's farm, Curtis Junior spied a field of grazing cows. All of a sudden, Curtis yelled out with great excitement, "Daddy, daddy, look at those great big dogs." Although we lived in Fort Worth, also known as "Cow Town," we never lived around where Cows were raised. After the excitement of seeing those great big dogs, we continued our journey.

A few miles further down the road, we came to a stretch of fields covered with fluffy white clouds as far as the eye could see.

We asked daddy to ask Uncle Fred to stop so we could get a closer look at this wonder. Daddy asked Uncle Fred to stop and soon Uncle Fred's sputtering old truck rolled to a stop and we jumped out and ran toward the fields of white clouds. We had never seen cotton growing.

We asked Uncle Fred if we could pick some and he told us to go ahead. We grabbed hands full and rubbed it against our face. It felt wonderful. Although mother had picked many a bag of cotton, she shared in our delight at being able to see cotton growing for the first time.

We finally arrived at Uncle Fred's place and settled in for a nice visit. His place was not a mansion, in fact, it was kind of run down but the hogs were fat and we had fun feeding them. All to soon our visit came to an end and we were on the rode back to the city. The next day was Easter Sunday and that meant getting ready for church. Mother's folks, just as did we, belong to the Church of God In Christ. The church they attended was known as "Bishop Mason's Church of God In Christ," which was a big two story red brick building, located in the colored section of Dallas.

On this particular Sunday, the church was putting on an Easter play entitled "The All Seeing Eye," complete with stage props, one of which was a metal box which Uncle Roy, my mother's oldest sister's husband, had fashioned into an illuminated eye. Uncle Roy was very good with his hands. I think it was Alfred, who recited a poem that morning, entitled The All Seeing Eye. Each time the all Seeing Eye was mentioned, the electric eye would blink. As I watched the eye blinking on and off, I thought how smart my uncle Roy was. He could do almost anything. He played the drums, cut hair, preached and made lots of things. What a day this was. The preaching, shouting and the music was a thing to behold. My cousin Roy Lee played his trumpet, Aunt Sister, her actual name Azalea, Roy Lee's mother, played the piano, as did my cousin Grace Lillian, Roy Lee's and Alfred's sister.

After many hours, the morning service ended and it was time to go back to Mama's for rest and a huge dinner before the evening service.

It was such fun being around my Aunts, uncles and my cousins. At Uncle Roy's, the men of the house engaged in an unusual form of entertainment, which involved the holding of farting contests.

To this day, I could never determine the rules of the game, other than if one messed in one's trousers, one would be instantly disqualified. The game appeared to be one of great spontaneity. Everyone would be quietly sitting around reading or otherwise engaged in some passive exercise and without notice or fanfare; the ambiance of quietness was suddenly shattered by a loud crackling noise, usually emanating from the direction of my Uncle Roy. This always brought about a round of laughter from the men and boys present.

My Aunt Sister, although used to these antics did not consider them to be funny and frequently made Uncle Roy aware of her displeasure, which appeared to make little difference to him and the other participants.

After much laughter, quietness was once again restored. All of a sudden, without notice or comment, Uncle Roy would once again break the silence with another loud crackle and this time he would say to Roy Lee "answer me son" and Roy Lee would raise one side of his bottom and another resounding fart could be heard throughout the house and then another and another back and forth they went.

It was a farting free-for-all. To this very day, when I think back of that day, it is difficult to keep my composure.

My mother's other sister, Blanche Easter, whom we called "Doll," was my favorite Aunt. She was pretty, young and daring. She played with us kids and seemed to enjoy it. She was one of the first colored females to join the Women's Army Corp (WAC).

Doll had already left for active duty on our last visit to Dallas. After Pearl Harbor was bombed and the possibility of women having to go overseas, she, along with other females were given the choice of being discharged or remain and take their chance. Doll decided to leave the service. She later moved to Ohio with the rest of the family, where she eventually Met and married Orland Jones.

My other aunt, Beatrice, whom we called Aunt Bea, was a self - educated missionary. If family history is accurately recorded, Aunt Bea must be recognized as a great woman of God. She dedicated her life to Jesus Christ and the church. She was saved at the age of 12 and knew no man other than Jesus Christ.

She served as a missionary in West Coast Liberia Africa for 20 years. She built churches, clinics, houses and several schools. There is much evidence of her work in the town of Tobak, Africa. She returned home when World War II broke out and went back after the war was over. She remained in Africa until ill health be failed her. She continued to work for the Lord by lecturing at various churches as long as her health allowed her to do so.

My mother's other brother, Willie Lott, known to us as Uncle Willie, worked and retired from the Telephone Company. We didn't see much of Uncle Willie because of the friction that existed between his wife, Stella and the rest of the family. Uncle Willie was a G.I. During WWII. One of the highlights of his service career occurred during his tour of duty overseas; he had an opportunity to play the piano to accompany Lena Horne, a popular colored singer. Uncle

Willie played the piano by ear. He could not read music. However, he played very well.

Fred E. Bolden, Ph.D

Chapter 3

Shortly after our last trip to Dallas, we moved from Rosedale Avenue to 1408 Louisiana. Louisiana was a beautiful tree-lined street with nice little houses. Daddy and mother had saved enough money to put a down payment on a house, which cost the exorbitant amount of $2,500.00. I thought we had moved into a mansion. Our home had a nice front porch with a swing that hung from the ceiling of the porch and a big back yard, which daddy fenced in. Our back porch was open but daddy enclosed it shortly after we moved in.

Daddy wanted us to be semi-independent in the area of our food supply so he bought several heads of chickens, which kept us supplied with eggs and fried chicken. In addition, he brought the goats, which he had acquired during our stay on Rosedale, which gave us goat's milk, the taste of which, you had to really get used to. The killing of chickens was left to mother.

I don't think she liked it very much, but she did it anyway.

Our new home had all the modern conveniences. Several gas stoves for heat and a large wood burner for cooking.

I remember our first winter. Daddy bought a supply of firewood and stock piled it on the back porch. One night as we slept, someone came onto the porch and stole most of our wood. I had never seen daddy so angry. God blessed us and he got another load of wood.

One of the problems with wood stoves was that they only heated one side of the body at a time.

I remember one very cold morning when we were all home from school. Daddy was not working because he had recently had his tonsils removed. Mother had gone to the store and daddy was in charge. Curt, my little sister, Faye and I were all huddled around the stove. The fire was going down so Curtis Junior attempted to put more wood in the stove. During the process, one of the embers from the stove fell on Faye's leg and slightly burned her. Daddy became furious. Although, he could not speak. Because of his surgery, he grunted and let Curtis Junior have a couple of licks across the back.

Living in our new home was fun for us three kids. Although, Curtis Junior and I didn't play much together and Faye was just a little girl, I quickly made new friends.

Winter passed and then came spring and finally summer and the 4th of July. Excitement ran high in anticipation of hearing and seeing the fireworks.

I remember it was two days before the fourth and there was a loud knock on our front door. Mother was ironing and appeared to be a little irritated because if she stopped ironing, she would loose the heat from her cast-iron irons, since we did not own an electric iron. These irons had to be heated on the stove. Usually, every home had at least two irons. You ironed with one while you heated the other one. There was a knock on the front door. Mother looked in the direction of the door and was visibly agitated.

It seemed that mother was not going to answer the door, but she carefully placed her iron on the stove and went to answer the door. As she approached the door, she saw that there was a white man standing on the porch at the door holding a large brown box in his arms. She reached the door and opened it and the man told her that he was selling firecrackers and wanted to know if she wanted to buy some of them. When I heard the word firecrackers, I yelled out to mother to please buy some, please buy some. She asked the man if he had small ones and how much they were. She told him that she did not want anything that would hurt her children. Mother was constantly telling us stories about people who had been seriously injured by firecrackers. As mother transacted with the man, she repeatedly inquired of him if the firecrackers were safe. The white man told her that they were so safe that they could be held in your hand and set off.

Mother paid the man and took the firecrackers. What happened next, I would not realize the impact of until I was a grown man.

After the man left, mother immediately went to the kitchen and took the box of wooden matches from the cupboard and went out on the back porch to test these hand-held firecrackers.

We anxiously followed her, thinking that we were going to light a few of them before the fourth of July. Such was not to be the case. I can see our wonderful mother standing on the back porch in the doorway removing one of these harmless little firecrackers from the string. She had taken a box of wooden matches, which she kept stored above our cooking stove, on her way to the back door. As she reached the door, she opened the screen door, removed one of the matches from the box and scratched its head on the doorpost and held its flaming end to the paper wick of the small firecracker. It sparkled and began to blacken. As soon the flame reached the small round paper covered black powder charge, the firecracker tore apart with a crackling sound, not like the big boom I had expected. Mother gave out with a yell as she grabbed her hand and started to blow on it.

The little firecrackers that the white man had told her was so safe that she could hold it in her hand had burned her.

Everything about mother suggested that she was a mild mannered Clark Kent (superman's other self), but she could become a tigress when necessary. Most of my lickings came from my mother. One of her favorites was to step on your foot and give you a little pinch and if that failed to get your attention, the old chinaberry switch would be the order of the day.

In addition to her motherly skills, mother played the piano and sang.

Mother, like most southern mothers, had a deep insight and understanding about her children. I remember one time when Mama, who was visiting us from Dallas, sent me to the store to buy her a bottle of coca cola. She gave me a quarter to buy the 5-cent coca cola, which was a lot of money, during those times. On the way to the store, I lost Mama's quarter.

I frantically searched all of my pockets but the quarter was gone. I looked on the floor of the store and up and down the street, but found no quarter. Finally, I reconciled myself to the fact that I would have to return home and break the news to Mama that I had lost her quarter.

I walked as fast as I could back down Louisiana toward home. My thoughts were mixed and filled with anxiety. I didn't know what to expect.

I arrived home and made my terrible announcement that I had lost Mama's quarter. I was pelted with the usual questions such as, are you sure you lost it? Did you look for it? And so forth.

Daddy flew into a rage and gave me a "whupping." To this day, I will never know if he punished me for the sake of impressing Mama, his mother in law or to teach me a lesson about lying or to train me to be more careful with money. Whatever his reason, I got it good.

My sweet mother drew me close to her, after my licking and slid her gentle hand into the pockets of my tattered pants hoping that the coin had eluded discovery and would be found. Her search, which was thorough, failed to turn up Mama's quarter, but she did discover a hole in one of my pockets large enough for several of her fingers to slide through. Mother, knowing her son, felt the matter should be investigated further. She took my fat little hand in hers as I continued to cry and we left the house in search of Mama's quarter. We left the house and took the same ill-fated route that I had previously taken.

As we neared the store, mother searched every crack in the sidewalk. As we neared a large vacant field, mother spied a shinny coin, which had lodged itself between the edge of the sidewalk and the weeds of the vacant field. Sure enough, there it was, she had found Mama's quarter. I was so happy that mother had found mama's quarter that I was no longer concerned about the unjust licking I had received from daddy. The one thing that my mother never asked me was if I had stolen Mama's quarter.

Upon our return home, mother jubilantly announced that she had found Mama's quarter. I don't remember daddy's reaction to the news but it was not one of sorrow for having given me an unjust licking.

As the years passed, I realize that there were plenty of times when I should have gotten a licking and didn't.

As I look back, I was a little on the mischievous side. I remember there was an older woman, about 30 or 35 years old, who lived next door to us.

She was in the habit of always leaving her shades up in her bedroom, which was right opposite our dining room window. This, in itself, was not bad. However, in addition to leaving her shades up, she would also undress with them in the up position. Being the precocious lad that I was, I would, with much stealth, slip into our dining room and perch myself in a position of vantage so that I might fill my eyes with the beauty of this disrobing female. Unfortunately, my newly found fantasy-maker was not to enjoy longevity.

Uncle Roscoe, one of my father's brothers, who was visiting us at the time, stumbled upon me while I was occupying my front row seat.

He chased me away and went and got my mother so that she could see what I had been exposed to. Mother promptly pulled down our shades and the following night when I returned for the nightly show, the theater was dark and the stage empty. It would appear that the curtain had come down on the final act and I was not to see another performance.

Alas, our neighbor's shades were drawn and the only thing I could see was shadows.

A major event was unfolding in the Bolden household. It was a hot August day in 1941 and mother was about to give birth to a new addition to the family. On August 9, 1941, daddy took mother to the hospital and when they returned home, they brought with them, my brand new little sister, Mary Elizabeth. For a ten-year-old boy, this was a big event. It was especially thrilling because I did not remember much about Faye's birth. Life in and around the Bolden house, after the birth of Mary was put on fast-forward.

When I was eleven years old, the folks decided it was time to leave The State of Texas. Our beautiful little house on Louisiana was put up for sale and sold. Mother and daddy started to make plans to move to some distant land known as Cleveland, Ohio, which was much further than Dallas.

After many weeks, the move started to take shape. Big boxes were collected and mother started to pack.

Like any excited kid, I went around telling everyone that we were moving way up north. The Barclays, my mother's oldest sister's family, had already made the move and were waiting for us to join them.

Daddy made the traveling arrangements for our family. His plan was to take my brother, Curt with him and mother, Fay, little Mary and myself would follow later. I begged daddy to take me instead of

Curtis junior but to no avail. I tried everything to get him to change his mind. I reminded him of something Curt had done and he had to get on him, but nothing made any difference, Curt was going and I was staying. I knew that my father loved me, but I always thought that he favored his firstborn over me. The days and weeks that followed crawled by painfully slow. At last the day came for our goodbyes to the Sovereign State of Texas.

The last of the Fort Worth Bolden's headed for the train station, bound for the land of dreams in Cleveland, Ohio. I had never seen or been inside of a train station. I couldn't believe the vast number of people gathered in one place to get on trains.

Just being in that large smoked-filled building was exciting for me.

I had never seen a real live train close-up before. Getting close to railroad tracks was another thing that mother had warned us about.

Each of us carried a bundle or a bag or two. Mother carried little Mary, whom she had carefully wrapped in a fresh baby blanket. We must have looked like a family of ducks, with mother in the lead and Faye and me following.

I remember us following mother to a little room in a remote section of the station with a sign over its door, which read "Colored." Mother directed me to go in and not to forget to wash my hands. I was so excited that I could hardly pee. When I left the toilet and went back into the giant station, I did not see mother and Fay. For a hot minute, I became very frightened, but as I turned and looked in the other direction, there they were. After all, I was to young to realize that ladies took more time in the toilet than us guys.

We returned to the long wooden benches located in the colored waiting section of the train station. Mother sat holding Mary and I was walking around the immediate area like a caged lion.

There was this loud monotone voice of the station Master announcing the arrivals and departures of various trains. I thought he had forgotten our train or we had missed it. It seemed like he called out every State and city except ours. Finally, the station Master's voice seemed to change. It became deeper and louder. He called out "Train for Cleveland, Ohio by way of St.Louis Missouri, now loading on track 14, all aboard!"

I jumped to my feet and grabbed my share of the bundles and was ready to go, but mother held me back and reminded me to look around and make sure that we had not forgotten anything.

Mother took one more last look and we headed in the direction of track Number 14. Mother instructed Faye and I to stay close to her so that we would not get lost.

Mother looked up in the direction of the various signs and saw the one that read tracks 14,15 & 16 and headed us in that direction.

As we approached the door that had Track 14 over it, we left the terminal and walked toward the big train, we were directed by a white man in a black suit toward the front of the line of coaches near the engine, which is where all colored passengers would be traveling, located directly behind the big coal burning, smoking engine. I thought this was one time that us colored folks could ride up front.

As we boarded the old coach, Faye and I clung close to mother as she weaved her way down a narrow isle in search of two empty seats. Mother took us to the rear of the coach so that we could be as far away from the smoke as possible. When we reached our seats, she directed me to turn one of the seats back so that we would be facing each other. I became instantly aware that our coach was very old and the seats were tattered and some of the hinges were broken.

We gathered our bundles around us and settled in for our long journey.

Mother held Mary with one hand and tried to make Faye and I comfortable with her other hand.

I could see that mother was very tired but she never complained. I asked her if I could hold Mary just for a little while, but she said no. I continued to beg her and finally she agreed but not until she had given me instructions on how to hold her properly.

Mother placed Mary on my lap. I felt pretty grownup holding my little sister and all. The old coach, in which we were riding, quickly filled with smoke as the engine made noises, which I thought meant we were on our way. Such was not the case. It was just the engine letting off steam and whatever else engines did. Suddenly, the entire train jerked and started to move. I couldn't believe it; we were finally on our way to Cleveland, Ohio.

The giant train began to pick up speed and was going faster and faster.

OREO

As the wheels of the train rolled along the long ribbons of steel, a strange percussion type melody seemed to filter through the tattered shade covered windows. The clackity clack sound became almost tranquilizing after a while. I noticed that mother had nodded off but the slightest movement by one of us, would cause her eyelids to partially separate. She made a quick check and dosed back off to an uneasy slumber. Mary was quietly sleeping in my arms as only an infant without a care in the world could do. Faye had snuggled against mother's lap and was sound asleep. I felt a deep urgency to stay awake and guard my sleeping family, which was tough.

The hypnotic effect from the sound of the clacking wheels made it even tougher to stay awake but I did. After a brief period, mother realizing that I was very sleepy, adjusted Faye on her lap and took Mary from me, which was the last thing I remembered until the conductor called out "Next stop St. Louis Missouri." Once again, mother started to get our things together using one arm and holding Mary with the other. I was dazed from having being awakened. Faye had her eyes open but she was still sleep. About a half hour later, the big train rolled to a stop and once again the conductor yelled out "St. Louis, St. Louis."

Fred E. Bolden, Ph.D

As soon as the train had stopped, people in our coach started to get up and move around. Mother told us to wait in our seats until the people behind us had moved past. As soon as the other people had left, we picked up our bundles and headed for the door of the coach.

We must have looked a sight. Our clothing were all wrinkled, hair not combed and sleepy eyed. The train station in St. Louis was very bright and large when compared to Fort Worth. It seemed like a city within a city. The one thing that struck me right away was the absence of those signs that read, "colored" or "colored only." The colored folks and the white folks were going into the same restrooms. We scarcely had enough time to go to the toilet before we heard the station Master's voice callout "The train for Cleveland, Ohio is now boarding on track 35, all aboard."

As we walked toward our track number, I looked around this massive structure of marble, glass, steel and glitter with great amazement and wonderment. I asked mother if we had time for me to have a drink of water. She nodded yes as we passed several drinking fountains. Once again, I was amazed that none of the fountains had signs over them identifying which one was for colored and which one was for white.

I was in for another surprise. As we approached our gate, I noticed that the white and colored passengers were entering the same coaches, which were larger and much more modern than the one's we had ridden in from Texas. After reaching our train, we followed mother to a set of beautiful plush seats, Mother gently placed Mary on one of the seats, put our stuff away and arranged our seats so that we faced each other.

The trip from St.Louis to Cleveland, seem shorter. Although, I was most anxious to see daddy and Curtis Junior, I sort of hated to see the trip end.

Chapter 4

July, 1942 the balance of the Bolden's arrived in the land of promise, Cleveland, Ohio. It was very late in the evening when we arrived and we were moving on low energy. The train station in Cleveland, Ohio did not impress me. It was dingy, poorly lighted and paled by comparison to St. Louis but looked much better than the one in Fort Worth, Texas. There was little activity in the station. None of that mattered, we were finally home and my heart was filled with great expectations and joy.

As mother looked around, I could tell that she was not the most excited person in the world about coming to Cleveland. She began to search for a sign that would direct us to a cabstand.

She headed us in the direction of a dimly lit corridor toward a set of exit doors.

Once again, without voicing it, I thought that Cleveland's train station was nothing like St. Louis." There were very few lights, no people, and no stores that were opened. Little did I know, that one day, I would find work in this very train terminal. The only place that showed some sign of life was a large room with a red, white and blue sign over its door that read USO. The terminal was so dead that the sign that read Western Union was off.

The Taxicab stand was located under a section of the terminal building where you could see the concrete pillars supporting the building. This area was also where passengers were dropped off and picked up. There were yellow cabs and checker cabs lined up waiting for fares. This would have been my first time ever riding in a taxicab. I learned later that mostly colored folks used the checker cabs and the white folks used the yellow cabs.

Mother directed us toward the first cab in line. The driver of the cab, a colored man, opened the doors for us and placed our bags and bundles in the trunk of the cab.

The cab driver was very courteous. He helped mother to get into the rear seat of the cab with Mary and Fay. I was allowed to sit in the front with the driver.

Mother gave the driver the address where Curtis and daddy were. The driver pushed down on a lever, which was attached to a clock-type meter on the dashboard of the cab and numbers appeared on its face, which represented the amount to be charged. The driver placed the cab in gear and we started to weave around the concrete pillars.

Soon, we immerged onto a street, which was almost as dark as had been the terminal.

As we left the terminal, we saw only a brief glimpse of what was downtown Cleveland.

After a short ride, we were away from downtown. The driver arrived at the address that mother had given him. Mother briefly looked around at what was definitely a slum area and asked the driver if he had the right street and address. The driver replied, "yes ma'am, this is East 29th & Scoville Avenue." Mother paid the driver. We got out of the cab and the driver unloaded all of our stuff.

Daddy, Curtis Junior, Cousin Perry and his wife, who owned the house, came out to meet us. Mother made a sincere effort at pretending to be glad to be in Cleveland, but her face clearly showed her disappointment. Not only was she unhappy with the house on East 29th Street, she was generally unhappy about the move to Cleveland.

From the look on mother's face, she was fully ready to return to Texas to our beautiful house on Louisiana.

After a round of hugs and kisses, our bags and bundles were carried into the house, if you could call it that. It was a typical run-down slum house.

Once we were alone, mother had an opportunity to talk to daddy. I noticed a tear on her cheek as she asked daddy to take us back to Texas. I couldn't hear what daddy said, but knowing him as I did, being bull-headed and all, no matter what mother said, we were here to stay and Cleveland, Ohio was going to be our new home.

Other than seeing Curtis Junior and daddy, nothing much happened on our first night. Mother unpacked a few of our things and we were hustled off to bed.

Our first morning in Cleveland, I woke up in a sort of daze. Light could be seen through the opaque or beige shades that covered our bedroom windows.

The early morning sunlight caused the darkness of night to fade as dawn approached. For an instant, as I awoke, I was lost in a strange place. After a few seconds, I realized that we were no longer in Texas and I instantly started to wake up everyone else. Other than eating, the only thing on my mind was seeing my cousin, Alfred.

The Barclays had rented a house directly across the street from where we were staying, which appeared to be in somewhat better shape.

I was excited and anxious to get the day started but mother, being tired and upset, told me to lie back down and don't disturb the rest of the house.

After a while, she knew it was no use. I was ready to get out of bed and that's all it was to it.

Everyone, except Curtis Junior, got up, dressed, washed and prepared to go and see the Barclays. I don't recall if we had breakfast at Cousin Frank's that morning or not. We left the house and walked across the street and up on the porch of the Barclay's house. I gave several anxious knocks on the front door and waited for it to open. The door did not open. I knocked again, much harder than before. Again we waited for the door to open. We knew they were home because it was Saturday and we had been told that people up north don't work on Saturdays. After a while, I heard rustling on the other side of the door and suddenly the door flung open and there stood my Aunt Sister and the rest of the household. I learned later, that the reason it took so long for them to answer the door was because they were so ashamed of their house and the neighborhood.

I had a ton of questions for my cousin, Alfred, who was visibly unhappy with their house but very glad to see me. At that moment, I could not have been happier because I could now spend all the time I wanted with my favorite cousin.

At that moment, Fort Worth, Mrs. Simpson's Boarding house, the Grand Theater and 1408 Louisiana Avenue didn't exist for me. I was here in Cleveland, Ohio with my cousin, Alfred. I didn't even mind that the next day was Sunday and I would have to go to church. Alfred showed me around the neighborhood and brought me up to date of what had been going on.

The first day went fast. As darkness settled over the litter-strewn street and its poorly kept dwellings, some of the inhabitants from the various houses started to gather in various small groups along the street. They were talking loud and drinking from bottles, which were inside of brown paper bags.

As I looked from my bedroom window, I could see other groups forming and doing the same thing. Their voices grew louder and louder and the language grew more coarse. I remember thinking was this where I was going to grow up? Did we leave our nice little home on Louisiana for this? I allowed myself to enter into fantasyland. I imagined that we had moved into a beautiful palace and all around us was nothing but beauty. I fell asleep with those thoughts in my mind.

Our first Sunday in Cleveland, Ohio was much like a Sunday in Texas, except mother did not have to cook; she was rushing around getting our things unpacked, while holding Mary on her hip. After we were all dressed, there was hardly enough time for breakfast, which was nothing like what we had been used to back home. After we had finished breakfast, mother made last minute checks on each of us, especially me since I always had to be reminded to tuck my shirttail in or brush some of my food that had fallen on my clothes. Even now, once in a while, when I brush crumbs from my suit after a meal, my memories go back to when mother had to remind me to do the same thing. Daddy was the driving force on Sundays. I can still hear him shouting out orders and asking mother if she was ready. Daddy was always very prompt throughout his entire active life; I guess that's where I got my propensity for always being on time. Finally, we were all ready to go and meet up with the Barclays.

Our journey started with a walk down East 29th Street toward Scoville Avenue and a short walk to East 30th Street, where we would catch a street car, which would carry us to downtown Cleveland.

After a brief wait, a rattling iron trolley approached us and stopped. I was filled with excitement and looked forward to riding on a streetcar for the very first time. The trolley was not quite like the train we had come from Texas in, but it was still fun to ride.

The trolley was very interesting. It was not operated by gasoline but drew its power from an electric line that ran down the street from overhead and was connected to the streetcar by a long metal pole with a roller at the end of it. A small coal furnace heated it with an electric blower, which generated very little heat during the cold winter and was tended by a conductor, who was seated near the middle of the coach. The seats were made of wicker and had no cushions on them.

After a short ride, we arrived at downtown Cleveland to East 4th Street and Prospect Avenue, where we were to transfer to another trolley. We got off the trolley and waited on a cement island for the trolley that would take us to our church.

Downtown Cleveland was a ghost town. Nothing was opened except a few restaurants.

Fred E. Bolden, Ph.D

After a short wait, my cousin, Alfred yelled out, "here it comes, the Woodland Street car." As the noisy iron trolley came to a stop, we all boarded it and headed for our new church, The Woodland Avenue Temple Church of God in Christ, located at 6812 Woodland Avenue. Woodland Avenue Temple was a neatly built structure of sandstone and brick, which was supposedly brought in by the pastor, Bishop Williams, a truckload at a time. As colored churches went, Woodland Avenue Temple was pretty nice. Our new church had wooden pews, not pieces of wood nailed together but real seats. The aisles were covered with runners of carpet and nice chandeliers hung from the ceiling. Many of the colored churches were located in old former retail stores. There are many of these churches still located in these former stores to this very day. The name that still identifies these churches is "Store-front churches." As we rode the trolley, I was so amazed with all of the steel tracks that ran down the center of the streets. After a short ride, our trolley stopped almost right in front of the church.

After a few Sundays of attendance, daddy was asked to preach, an offer he gladly accepted. As Jackleg preachers (preachers without formal education) went daddy was an excellent preacher. In fact, I enjoyed his preaching. I could understand what he was preaching about. I must admit, I did not care for Holiness or Church of God in Christ preachers. They yelled and hollered and I seldom understood what they were preaching about.

My dad's preaching was different, not just because he was my dad, but because he was a natural teacher-type preacher, who had the ability to make himself, understood.

I was very proud of my father's preaching ability. He was articulate, biblically accurate, as I understood it and was given a lot of "Amen's," when he preached.

After we had settled into our new church, The Boldens and Barclays became the foundation of the music for the church.

My cousin Roy Lee and I played the trumpet, Alfred played the Saxophone, Grace Lillian, Sister and my mother played the piano and Uncle Roy played the drums.

Our church was a great church. Once each month we would broadcast over the radio. It was on one of these broadcasts that I made my debut as a Gospel singer. I sang "Precious Lord."

Fred E. Bolden, Ph.D

As I reflect back, the only time I had ever heard of Cleveland was when we used to listen to a choir on the radio by the name of "Wings over Jordan," They were terrific.

Attending church wasn't all that bad. One of the high points was stopping after church at the hot dog stand located on East 4th & Prospect for a delicious hotdog and a soda water (pop).

Although, I enjoyed those hotdogs, they were nothing like the ones we used to get in Texas. There was a makeshift hotdog stand on Rosedale Avenue, operated by some Mexicans. The size of the hotdogs they sold was double in size to the ones in Cleveland and was topped with the best chili in the world. We seldom had a chance to get those hotdogs because they cost 15 cents each, to much money for us.

Our stay on East 29th Street turned into weeks and then months. It seemed that we were doomed to be slum dwellers for the rest of our lives.

Little did I know that daddy had been shopping for a house for us. I should have known that my daddy would not allow us to live in housing such as where we were. Daddy finally found us a "new" home. It was an old house in a changing Jewish neighborhood, located in a part of town known as "Jew Town also The Gold Coast."

Our new house was much larger than we needed. It had three floors plus a basement.

Daddy was a very giving man with illusions of grandeur and the heart of a philanthropist with the pocketbook of a pauper. His spiritual gifts were definitely the gifts of giving and teaching.

Daddy gave of his talents, what little money he had, and most of all, he gave of himself. He was a contemporary visionary who truly believed that anything was possible through prayer and hard work. I must admit that he endowed in me a healthy dose of the same traits, as I did to my sons, Allen and Fred, II. My other son, Orville, works only as much as he has to.

Mother was not totally in agreement with daddy's choice for our house. Mother had been used to our little family house in Texas and didn't want such a large house, but daddy being the headstrong person that he was, bought it anyway.

After several weeks of daddy and mother making the necessary financial arrangements, the Bolden's, Barclays and Mama moved in our "new" Cleveland home at 1148 East 99th Street.

The Barclays were going to live with us until they found a home of their own. They lived on the first floor and we lived on the second floor. The Barclays later moved into the parsonage of the Olivet Church of God in Christ, which was located south of our house on East 99th street, several blocks away. They ultimately moved into their own home on East 92nd Street near the culture gardens and right across the street from Miles Standish, the elementary school, from which I graduated.

There were very few colored families living in the area when we first moved in. East 99th Street was a beautiful street arched by giant maple and oak trees that grew leaves in such profusion that during the summertime you could not see from one end of the street to the other.

The Abraham's, from whom daddy and mother bought our house, had put very little in the upkeep of the property. It was still a great house. It had beautiful highly polished oak columns separating the living room from the dining room, leaded glass windows; marble encased fireplaces and still remaining were Jewish prayer scrolls on each entry doorpost.

In addition, it had two big nasty coal burning furnaces, from which Curtis Junior and I was afforded the opportunity and pleasure of emptying box after of box of ashes. I would often, no not often, but always rebel when told to empty out the ashes from the furnace. I was a very lazy boy when it came to any housework. My specialty was eating, playing and sleeping. I guess you could have considered me the great outdoors type. Daddy ultimately had the furnaces converted to gas, for which I was most happy.

There was an industrious side to my nature, which was somewhat redeeming. I liked to work outside of the home at any job I could find.

I got my first job when I was 8 years old. I sold the Pittsburgh Courier, a colored publication in the Fort Worth, Texas area. When I was 10 years old, I got a job at a commercial laundry operating a giant mangle. When Chinese checkers were first introduced, my brother Curt and I were given a job at Woolworth's where daddy worked at the time, playing Chinese checkers in the window of the store. They dressed us in Chinese clothing. How about that two black Chinamen. In addition, I waited on tables and mopped floors at Simpson's Boarding house, which was daddy's main job. I even worked for a blind man, who collected papers and old rags for salvage. My last job was working for a men's clothing store, which I took over from Curtis when daddy and he left for Cleveland. Speaking about being lazy, I remember one time when daddy told me to take a bath, which I could not work into my playing time. I protested in a manner befitting my young years. I finally told my daddy that I would take a bath if he filled the tub with water. He hit the ceiling. My response to his uncompromising attitude was, well, you're the one who want me to take a bath. I knew not to push my luck any further. I filled the tub and jumped in.

My brother Curt was a little on the lazy side too however, he was neat and clean about himself and was more proactive about helping mother around the house. The one thing Curt and I hated in common was being forced to help daddy with his unending rebuilding the house projects. From the moment we moved in, daddy formulated plans to make our home into a mini-Simpson's Boarding house. As far as I was concerned, the best thing he ever did in our home was turned those coal burners into gas, which eliminated the need for coal bins and taking out the ashes. Even that change brought on more work for us. With the conversion of the coal furnaces to gas, we no longer needed coal bins, as such; daddy got another vision of converting the former coal bins into living quarters, which he promptly did. Eventually, after many modifications, two kitchenettes, garden level, of course, rose from the dust and dirt of two former coal bins.

Daddy's efforts and architectural genius became a source of amusement for years to come. One of my brothers in law's friend dubbed daddy "King Kitchenette." Mother vigorously objected to daddy's house conversion efforts, but as usual, it made no difference. He went full speed ahead with hammer flying and saw blade whirling. One of mother's main objections was daddy bringing in so many strangers into the house. Daddy always looked at the economic side of his efforts. The strangers would bring in much needed revenue, which he put right back into his building projects. I don't think daddy ever realized a Penney's profit from all his efforts, except he helped a lot of people. By the time daddy had used up all available space, we wound up with some 28 rooms. By the time daddy hammered his last nail, put in his last pipe and screwed his last screw, 1148 East 99th Street was practically rebuilt. I am somewhat amused that since my nephew, Ronald Jones, my sister Faye's son, who was left the property, has taken over, he has changed all that daddy did. Although, his changes are much different than daddy's, the old house looks great.

Fred E. Bolden, Ph.D

Chapter 5

Much happiness and some sorrow were to become a part of the heritage of this old house. Our first summer living on the Gold Coast was most exciting. I remember, shortly after we moved in, I was sent to the store to buy some lunchmeat. The main shopping area was on East 105th Street. In order to get to East 105th Street, I had to walk down Westchester or South Boulevard, which were side streets leading off of East 99th Street. As I casually strolled down South Boulevard, I gazed about me at some of the old houses with Jewish families sitting on their front porches talking to their neighbors and family members. I could almost feel their eyes following me as I passed each house. Colored families were still a novelty in the neighborhood.

East 105th Street, during those days, hosted a variety of small shops, grocery stores, two synagogues and two delicatessens, which when the wind was just right, gave of an aroma of cooking corned beef, the likes of which would tantalize the most discriminating of palates.

It was this pleasurable culinary bouquet that drew me to Perkins's Delicatessen, a delightful Jewish establishment.

I was given five dollars, a lot of money, to buy some lunchmeat and bread. Lunchmeat, to me, was what I smelled, so I spent the entire five bucks on Corned Beef. Corned beef, even then, was expensive. As such, what I bought was hardly enough to feed 11 people, who represented all of the family plus those who had help us move. When I returned home with my small grease seeping package of sweet saver, everyone was delighted with its pleasant aroma but very displeased with the quantity.

Uncle Roscoe, who was one of the movers, took me back to the deli and returned the meat and explained to the owner that I was just a young boy and did not realize the limited amount of corned beef that $5.00 would buy. The unwilling but understanding clerk took back the meat and refunded our money, which was then spent on several pounds of bologna and two loaves of bread.

Our family settled in and started the routine of living in our new home. As the curtain of summer started to fall, nature began to change its props. The leaves on the giant Maple trees began to take on shades of yellow and orange and a tinge of brown. The sight was breath taking to watch the leaves fall to the ground cascading themselves into a carpet of various colors, the likes of which only Mother Nature could make. I will never forget the pure joy of walking through the park kicking through the piles of leaves. Once in a while, we would jump into the piles of leaves that had been heaped up in front of various houses.

Summer faded into fall and the start of school. I would be going to a brand new school with kids that were very different from me. I was the only colored person in my room and the biggest. Curtis and my dear cousin, Alfred would be going to other schools and I wanted to be with them. I had a year to go in elementary school.

The first day that mother took Faye and I to school, I was more frightened than excited. We left home early on a Monday morning and walked to Miles Standish Elementary School, which was a one-story brick building very well kept.

As we entered the building, I became even more apprehensive. I didn't see one colored face.

We were directed to the principal's office, where we were registered and turned over to an office clerk, who took us to our various rooms.

Because of my large size and precocious nature, I felt awkward and out of place with the other kids. The teacher introduced me to my classmates and directed me to a seat. I promptly folded my hands, placed them on top of my desk, remained still and erect and said nothing to anyone except to acknowledge his or her childish efforts at trying to make me feel comfortable and welcome.

I don't remember learning very much in the 6th grade but I do remember my constant feelings of superiority over those little kids in my class. I just couldn't understand why the school couldn't realize that I should not be there but in a school with kids more mature, like myself.

After an eternity, graduation came and finally I would be with kids my size. The Junior high school that I would be attending was known as Empire Junior High School. I would now be a "Flat," which was the name given to new 7th graders. I never did learn what the term meant, I was just happy to be one.

Fred E. Bolden, Ph.D

Our neighborhood started to change rapidly after we moved in, as did the school. There were some fights but for the most part, integration went reasonably smooth. Most of my sixth grade class did not come with me. Their families moved on to another Jewish neighborhood.

I played in the band and did very well. In fact, I was so good that Mr. Klein, my music teacher, who was also the bandleader at Glenville High School, drafted me to play the tuba, although my primary instrument was the trumpet, at one of Glenville's football games. By the end of my second year at Empire, I was ready to call it quits. I was told about a school called Cleveland Trade School that I could attend after completing the 8th grade. I gathered all the information about the school and presented the plan to the folks.

I was happily surprised when they went for it.

Daddy took me to sears and bought me a toolbox complete with various tools. I never really wanted to be a mechanic I just wanted change. Many times, I wished my parent had not allowed me to transfer.

The mechanic's class was a joke. I couldn't drive and disliked getting my hands greasy. What I really wanted to do was quit school.

While at Cleveland Trade School, I met a boy by the name of Norman Brown, who worked after school at a flower shop known as Kuntz Flower Shop, which was located several blocks from the school. I asked him if he could get me a job there and he stated that he would try. One day, right after school, he took me with him. I was introduced to a gray haired old man, by the name of John Kuntz, the owner. I hung around the shop for the rest of the day doing everything I could to impress the owner. I swept the floor, ran errands and made a couple of deliveries on the streetcar. I was hired. My pay was 75 cents per hour. I was very happy with the arrangement. I was now an independent person with my own money.

The money was not great, even in those days, but it was a job. After work, I went home and told mother about the job and she was happy for me.

Each day, right after school, I would head for the flower shop. I was taught how to clean the dead leaves from the flowers and arrange them in the display cooler. I washed the front windows and was taught how to decorate them. After working a few months, I was allowed to try my hand at flower arranging. Although, I didn't care for the work, I became pretty good at it. The Kuntz' were Jewish and catered to a lot of Jewish weddings, which meant that I had to work a lot of Sundays, the day Jewish people got married.

Mr. Kuntz, was a very difficult man to work for, He had two main interests in his life, betting on sports, primarily the horses and satisfying his overactive libido. It was not uncommon for ladies of the street to frequent the shop during the day for the purpose of servicing his special sexual needs.

His strong compulsion to gamble took him away from the business every afternoon, leaving me in charge to attend to the business, which involved sales, design and sometimes servicing some of his female friends.

My dreams went far beyond the flower shop. In fact, I grew to hate it.

I had four main ambitions for my life; I wanted to be a policeman, fly an airplane, teach school and be a soldier. I think my desire to be a policeman started when I was an elementary school-crossing guard, which I felt was a great honor. I enjoyed wearing my AAA silver badge and the white garrison belt that went with it.

Shortly after I turned 15, my cousin, Alfred and I went downtown to sign up for the army. I made all the arrangement as far as school was concerned. I lied and told the school I was going to a military school and would be transferring. I told the recruiting officer that I was 17 years old. Somehow, mother and daddy got wind of my plan and when I arrived at the recruiting office, I was sympathetically turned away. I cried bitter tears and vowed that I would run away from home.

After my efforts to join the army were thwarted, I joined the Civil Air Patrol, since I wanted to learn how to fly. Although, the Civil Air Patrol did not offer me the opportunity to fly, at least, I was around pictures of airplanes. A year later, once again, I lied about my age and joined the 372nd Infantry Battalion of the Ohio National Guard, which was an all colored unit. This time I got away with putting my age up. I was sworn in and issued a set of uniforms. All of us new recruits were given a stern lecture about attending meetings and being prompt. My commanding officer was Frederick M. Coleman, who at the time was a mail carrier in civilian life and also a law student. Years later, he became a judge and a U.S. Attorney and my best friend up to the day he passed away.

Being accepted in the National Guard was truly a high point in my life.

Fred E. Bolden, Ph.D

My unit met in an old building that had been converted into an armory. The white units had modern armories located on the Westside and far eastside. We trained every Tuesday from 7 PM to 10 PM and I never missed a training schedule. What a joy it was for me to wear my uniform. Each summer we would go to Camp Perry, an army camp near Sandusky, Ohio, which had formerly been used for German prisoners, for weapon's training and once a year we would go to a regular army camp for two weeks of field training.

My vacations away from the flower shop were spent at an army camp and I loved every minute of it. We soldiered all day and when we weren't on a detail, we were allowed a pass to go into the nearest town for fun and games.

As a boy or young man, all of my associates were older than me, both male and female. When it came to females, lying about my age became a way of life. I would tell them that I was in the regular army, not the National Guard. Sometimes, I would put on my uniform after getting off of work from the flower shop and just parade around in it.

Chapter 6

It was during this era that I met the girl that would become my first wife.

Emma Genevieve Robinson, who was a ticket girl at a neighborhood theater, known as the Crown Theater, which was located on the lower or northern end of East 105th Street. Emma, hailed form Flint Michigan and as fate would have it, my second wife was also from the state of Michigan. Emma was as cute as a bug in a rug, had a wonderful personality and was five years older than me. Needles to say, I became a regular patron of the Crown Theater. I was bound and determined that I was going to make out with her. I saw the same movies over and over many times.

Finally, my persistence paid off and she gave me her address, which was right around the corner from the picture show on a street known as Morrison Avenue. Although Emma was 22 years old at the time, she had somehow managed to keep herself virtuous, even though she had many men pursuing her.

I knew I had my work cut out for me, if I was to be successful in competing with my male peers, who were not really my peers, because all of them were much older than me.

I drew from my bag of deceptive tricks all that were available; I used a deeper voice, I was stern, but pleasant and spoke only on adult-type topics.

Emma lived with her mother, two older sisters and two brothers. Their family life style was very different than that of my family. Their housekeeping left a lot to be desired. Her mother, Mrs. Vashti Robinson, a tiny, hard workingwoman, was the mainstay for the family and did all that she could to keep her family together. Shortly after Emma and I starting dating, her family moved to a house several blocks from where they lived to a house on Garfield Avenue.

After many dates and visits to her house, we both lost our claim to sexual purity. Before Emma, I had played around a bit but never had engaged in any real sex. Those first few experiences with Emma gave me an entirely new outlook on life. I was like a kid being turned loose in a candy store and told to get whatever he wanted.

Although, Emma was five years older than me, her child-like mannerisms, made her appear much younger.

I began to spend more and more time at her house and less and less time at my house. A few months before my 16th birthday, I impregnated Emma. I was bewildered, frightened and didn't know where to turn or what to do. Finally, I had to tell mother and daddy what I had done.

The two families got together for a discussion but nothing was resolved. Her family and me decided that we should get married but marriage involving a juvenile was prohibited by law. As such, the marriage had to be approved by a juvenile court judge.

I was more concerned that my lying had caught up with me and now it had to all come out in the open that I was an overgrown kid.

A court date was set before Judge Harry Eastman, a well-known and tough judge, who had sent many a youngster away.

Daddy knew how such a marriage would turn out and was not shy when it came to expressing his opinion. In fact, there was a heated discussion between him and Mrs. Robinson just before we all went into the courtroom.

Mrs. Robinson was very supportive of the marriage and offered her support in any way that she could.

Judge Eastman was not happy with the situation or us. His opening remarks were somewhat disturbing, especially when he threatened to send us both away, Emma for contributing to the delinquency of a minor and me for juvenile delinquency. To say I was scared, didn't begin the tell the story. My mental anguish was dispelled when the judge relented and gave his permission, after giving us a stern lecture.

Due to my very young years, even after my father's objections and the judge's admonishing lecture, I still didn't fully understand or even accept the seriousness of our act, in fact, I was sort of happy. A few days later, Emma and I went for a blood test and then to the courthouse for a license. I will never forget the look on the clerk's face when I told her my age.

She promptly informed me that I was to young and could not be issued a license to marry. I then smugly and confidently presented her with the court order. She had never been confronted with a situation like this before so she took the court order and gave it to her supervisor who told her to issue the license.

Several days later, in the presence of her family and mine, we stood before Reverend Robinson, no relation to Emma, and were joined together as "man" and wife. The ceremony took place at daddy's house.

Our wedding was simple and with little fanfare. Emma was already showing. She wore a cloth topcoat, on which I attached a gardenia corsage. After the celebration, we had cake and punch. After the wedding, we moved in with Mrs. Robinson and her family. Mrs. Robinson's house was unkempt and poorly organized, nothing like the home I had been used to, but there was a lot of love in the house.

I completed my course work at Cleveland Trade School and went to work fulltime at the flower shop. The Kuntz' paid me $75.00 per week, before taxes, which left me with $62.50 take-home. As far as I was concerned, the only good thing about my job was when I would go to lunch, I would buy a couple of hotdogs and go to one of the area shows, which meant that most of the time I would return back to work late. The next day, I would do the same thing. Mr. Kuntz would scold me, but I kept right on doing it. I guess the reason that he did not fire me was he knew he was getting me cheap.

During Emma's pregnancy, I did all the things an expectant father was supposed to do. Such as, slipping out of the house late at night to get Emma some watermelon or a bag of chocolate chip cookies or whatever else she might have wanted. My paradise away from home was to be short lived. A few weeks later, after Emma and I had settled in at Mrs. Robinson's house, we had a couple of surprise visitors. Mother and daddy came over. Apparently, Emma's sister, Grace, spied them as they approached the house and alerted the rest of the family. The greetings by the Robinson family were cordial enough, under the circumstances. Mother and daddy were invited in a directed to have seats on a used couch that Mrs. Robinson had purchased a few days before. It was a nice day so mother and daddy had walked over from East 99th Street.

The gathering was cordial enough but was definitely dominated by daddy. Daddy had one thought in mind and that was to get his son out of that house and back home. Although the meeting was not long, the end result was what daddy wanted. Several days later, I packed my few things and my very pregnant wife and moved back home. Daddy moved us on the third floor of the house, which had been previously occupied by my brother, Curtis Junior, who was more than a little displeased with the arrangement.

I assured him that I would only be there a short time and he would have his room back. A short time turned out to be 10 years. On July

13, 1948, I rushed Emma to University hospital's McDonald House, where she gave birth to our first son, whom we named Allen Wensted Earl Bolden. I didn't have the money to pay for the hospital, which was $125.00. As such, the hospital allowed me to make payments. I was very happy with our new son, but my happiness was not like that such as a new father would have experienced, but it was like unto that of a little boy who had done something he was not supposed to do and gotten away with it. Because of my youth, I was not in on very much of Allen's early raising. For that matter, neither was Emma. She worked and I stayed in the streets. Mother and daddy did most of the raising. Two years later, Allen was followed by another son, whom we named Orville Lavere, who was born June 20, 1950. Orville did not have the luxury of being born in a fancy hospital; he was born on the third floor of daddy's house with me acting as assistant midwife. Seeing a human being come into the world was mind-boggling. If anyone does not believe in the miracle of creation as a wonder of God, being a part of birth should change his or her mind.

By the age of 18, I had sired two children and was doing a very poor job of being a father and husband. Right along about then, many of the things daddy had warned me about had long reached fruition.

I had already begun to loose interest in Emma and I'm sure she felt the same way. I looked around at some of the kids I had gone to school with and many of them were getting ready to go to college. I was a big boy trapped in a man's responsibility. All of The things daddy had warned me about, way back when I was 15 years old kept coming back in my mind. I wasn't married a year and was already seeking other pastures in which to graze. I remember my early child-thinking. Such as, our love would last forever because we were so much in love. Boy! Was daddy ever right?

I was barely 18 when an opportunity presented itself for me to stray from the marital bed. On this particular occasion, the flower shop was about ready to close for the day and Mr. Kuntz received an order for flowers. I heard him tell the customer that he could deliver the flowers the same day. I knew this meant working later. No matter where the order was to go, Mr. Kuntz always figured it was on my way home. After the order was completed and packed, I started for the bus line that would carry me and the cumbersome package to the customer's house. On the way, the only thing I could think of was how much I hated my boss and my job. After what appeared to be hours, I arrived at my stop. I got off the bus and walked toward the address that was on the label. White people still largely inhabited the houses in this area. The bus was very crowded and I was glad to get off of it. As I walked toward the customer's house, I remembered having the same thoughts I had when we moved in our house on East 99th Street. White people were sitting on their porches and I thought that all of them were staring at me. This made me even angrier.

After a long walk, I finally reached the house. It was an old two-story frame house, pretty much like the one we lived in. I walked up the sidewalk leading to the house and up several steps to the front door. I rang the doorbell. There was no immediate response so I rang the bell again. This time I pushed the bell button harder and longer, expressing my anger at being kept waiting. What seemed to be minutes later, the door opened and there stood a buxom, milk white lady with carrot red hair and a big smile. She apologized for having kept me waiting and with a waive of her hand, she invited me in.

The front entrance led into a large and cluttered living room, filled with packing boxes on the floor and on top of very old-styled furniture. The walls were adorned with old yellowing photographs encased in oval frames. She closed the front door behind me and instructed me to follow her.

As we weaved our way through the clutter of boxes, which had been packed with glassware, dishes, towels and other household items, she explained that she was in the process of packing in anticipation of moving. This area, like most on the near eastside was changing and all the white folks were running. She directed me to her kitchen and asked me to arrange her flowers in a vase. She cleared away some of the cans of food and boxes that were lined up on the table. I agreed to do so only because I thought I might receive a tip. I requested a sharp knife and her vase. After I had arranged the flowers she had me set them on her old style buffet in the dining room.

As I placed the flower arrangement on the buffet, I noticed several stacks of dirty books. After she was sure that I had seen the covers, she asked me to sit down, which I did. The old chair was most comfortable but I could not get my mind off of those books. She asked me how long I had been working for Johnny Kuntz and in my older man's voice I responded with, I had been there so long that I no longer remembered.

We continued to make small talk and she finally got around to what she wanted to really talk about. She asked me if I was married and I told her that I was. My answer went right over her head as if I had said nothing or no. She gave me several of her dirty books to read and look at the pictures. I want to tell you, they really got me primed. The next thing I knew, I was being led to her bedroom.

By the time we reached her high four posted bed, I was void of all clothes.

Doris Hubbard, her name was a 50-year-old widow, who apparently spent most of her time eating, reading dirty books and making love, which was OK by me. During my early youth, I was very taken my full-bodied older women. In fact, they were the objects of many of my sexual fantasies. After this encounter with Doris, I frequently and cheerfully delivered flowers to her house. On several occasion, I just delivered me.

The day came when Doris finally sold her house and moved to parts unknown. Each year after she moved, I would search the telephone books to see if her name and number would pop up, but alas no such luck. During the next few years, I further fulfilled my daddy's prophecy in its entirety. Doris was the first of many to come.

Chapter 7

What I call my other life began after I turned 21 years old. I decided that I was getting nowhere fast and needed an education. I wanted to become a commissioned officer in the National Guard and that required a minimum of a high school diploma, plus I was a rotten mechanic and hated the flower business.

Once I took a side job of repairing a person's car. I messed his car up so badly that he sold it and bought another one. This was my first and last effort at being a mechanic. During this time in my life, I was also taking flying lessons. I would take the bus or I should say several busses to the airport, since I could not drive yet, nor did I have a car.

I took my first flying lesson on Sunday May 15, 1950. That was truly a happy day for me. I had a tough time getting into a flying school since most or all of them were highly segregated and did not want colored students. Richland School of Aviation, the school that did accept me, did so only after the instructor told me that as a colored flyer, I would never get a job. The only reason he took me was the color he recognized most was green, the color of money.

I was told the price of each lesson and within the hour my instructor and me were airborne. I was too dumb to realize that I was being taken advantage of by not getting some ground school first. I was just happy to be in an airplane and would be soon in the air at the controls of a real one.

Dutifully, I reported each and every Sunday for my flying lesson. I took to flying like a duck to water. Those Sunday mornings were like being in a little part of God's heaven. When I taxied down the runway for a take off, I imagined I was a member of the Flying Tigers or the 99th Pursuit squadron, a black flying unit during WWII out of Tuskegee, Alabama.

Finally, after my 14th hour of dual instruction, my instructor felt that I was ready to take my first solo flight. My instructor, that day, was a devilish WWII Army Air Corp pilot of Italian descent. I remember him saying to me; are you ready to do it alone? I replied with a loud AH Roger. My heart skipped a couple of beats when he told me to land and let him out.

I made a magnificent landing, pulled off of the apron and let him out.

I taxied to the end of the strip in preparation of my first solo flight and when I got into position, I forgot everything I had been taught.

I nervously gave the tower my position and told them I was ready for takeoff. They replied Cessna 155, the identification number of the plane I was flying, you are clear for an immediate takeoff. I poured on the coal and before you could say Lord have mercy, the wheels of my plane were off the ground. I made several turns around the field and made preparation for my first solo landing.

It was a perfect three-point landing. I taxied over to where my instructor was. As I approached him and brought my plane to a stop, he grabbed the wing of my plane and shook it. He opened the cockpit door and congratulated me. He got back in the plane and we taxied back to the hanger line, where he signed my official logbook as a licensed student pilot.

Although, I was now considered a student pilot and had learned the basics, I knew I had a lot to learn about navigation and the physiology of flying, so I decided to look for another flying school. I found one in Chagrin Falls, Ohio, known as Horne's Flying School.

Horne's was a very small field located on the outskirts of Chagrin falls, Ohio, taking its name from a natural fall, which was located in the town. The airport at Chagrin Falls was surrounded by tall trees and had all grass runways.

My first day on the field, was far more comfortable than my first day at Cleveland Airport. The instructors acted as if they really wanted me to be there. My first flight from this little field was just as exciting as my first flight at Cleveland. After all, I was now a student pilot, you know, a real expert (funny). I quickly found out that flying from a small field was very much different that those big fancy concrete runways I had been used to. Flying from a field surrounded by tall trees made you wanting to be as close to God as possible. Landing was something else. You had to come in at treetop level and slip (loose altitude fast while maintaining a straight descending glide path by using the controls in an opposing manner) the plane in for a landing. This was a tricky maneuver. I mastered the technique quite easily and was very proud of myself. After many hours of ground school and dual flight, I was finally ready for my first cross-country flight. I had to fly to two other cities. One leg of the flight had to be at least 100 miles long.

I was nervous but ready. The weather was marginal and although I was about to poop in my pants from being nervous, I was going.

My instructor gave me some final instructions concerning the weather. In as much as my initial flight path would take me by Cleveland Hopkins, I was to fly below the weather but stay out of the traffic pattern, which was 600 feet, once I reached Cleveland.

As I approached Cleveland, I dropped to about 1,000 feet while attempting to maintain my heading and the proper altitude. Just when I thought everything was just fine I looked off to the north, toward Lake Erie, lo and behold, I spied a giant DC-3, considered a large airplane at the time, which I thought was coming right for me.

I poured on the coal, pulled back the stick and started to climb. I climbed right into the overcast, where I was told to stay out of. I lost control and froze on the stick. I had the stick full back in my belly. I knew that was a mistake but I was scared of that DC-3. Having that stick back at that speed was the worst thing I could have done, as it put the plane in a power stall. Sure enough, the plane went into a spiraling power stall and started down. It was then that something strange happened, I heard a voice, which had to be the voice of God, although I was not saved at the time; it told me to just let the controls go and everything would be OK. I did just that. After releasing the stick, the plane went into an automatic gradual descent and I was once again in control.

On this particular day, I was flying a Piper Cub, which is a very forgiving plane and was used by many schools. To this day, I thank God that he allowed me to regain my composure. That was a good thing. I was just about to crash into the Bomber plant, which is now the IX Center. I made the necessary corrections and started a normal climb and followed the lake back to Chagrin falls, Ohio. When I finally reached my home base, the news had already reached them. This sad series of events meant that I would have to take cross-country flying all over again. I didn't care what had happened, I was a pilot and had accomplished one of my major life's goals. I didn't do much flying after that. I knew it was time to stop fooling around and get a real education. I decided to go back to school and compete a regular high school, in as much as trade school taught one a trade but did not give you a high school diploma. Since I had to work, I made plans to attend high school at night. The school closest to me was John Hay High School. The following Monday, I went to John Hay and registered for classes. I felt good the moment I stepped into the registrar's office.

There is something about being in a learning environment that makes you feel instantly smarter. My class was well mixed with white and colored students.

I sat opposite a white female, who had the appearance of an old maid, but was very attractive, or could be, and extremely reserved.

I spoke to her and introduced myself as she extended her hand and told me that her name was Josephine Klusak. I didn't know why, but I felt somewhat attracted to her. It might have been that I was vulnerable at the time because of no longer having good old Doris anymore. The one thing I did know was that I no longer saw in Emma the things I saw in her when I was 15 years old. It had gotten so that any time I spent at home was to take a bath and get ready to be with someone else. After meeting Josephine, I filed the introduction away in the back of my mind with a mental bookmark to check into it further later.

Classes were held three nights per week and I tried to never miss a class. A few weeks passed and on one Wednesday night after class, I asked Josephine if she would like to stop for a sandwich and a coke.

She instantly replied that she would love to. Our class had another few minutes before it was over but I was now getting anxious. Right after class we walked down East 107th Street to Walgreen's drug store, took us a booth and ordered our food and drinks. We talked about everything from nationally foods to race relations. Josephine was 40 years old, estranged from her husband and of Czechoslovakian descent. She shared with me that her husband was an active member of the communist party and had gone under ground because of Senator Keifauffer's committee that was currently investigating all subversive groups and many were going to jail.

After several dates, we started to see each other before and after class. She eventually invited me over to her home, which was located on the south side of Cleveland on a street known as Pershing Avenue. Going to 5051 Pershing Avenue, proved to be a challenge, in that it was located on a double lot, front and rear with her parents living in the rear house. These were still pretty tough times for mixed couples. It was bad enough for a white woman to date a colored man, but much worse if the white woman was of foreign descent. The southeast side of Cleveland was predominantly ethnic. The only colored in the area were those passing through or working in the area. Obviously, I was neither.

At the end of my second semester at John Hay, I was offered an opportunity to go on active duty in the military, so that I could attend leadership school at Fort Benning Georgia, The Infantry School (TIS). This was indeed another high point in my life, which I couldn't pass up.

It was January 1952. I made arrangements for a leave of absence from my job and shortly thereafter, I received my orders and headed south. The train ride down to Columbus, Georgia was pleasant enough, but once in Georgia, many of my old memories returned and I felt the full weight of what it was like to be south of the Mason-Dixon line. I began to spot the signs of the white man's resistance to change, which I considered, as monuments to his stupidity. Every where you looked were the old signs "Colored Only" or "White Only." I grabbed my duffle bag and footlocker and preceded to walk toward the colored waiting room, just as mother, Faye and little Mary and I had done years before in Texas and waited for the bus that would take me the rest of the way to Fort Benning, Georgia. I had not been away from the south so long that I didn't know how to act. I fell right in line. The bus for Fort Benning arrived shortly after the train pulled in and although I had to go to the toilet, I held it. I refused to take a step back in time after having lived up north for several years.

1952 was a special year for military personnel. President Truman had ordered that all military troops be integrated. I was pleased with this order. We, as children were blessed being raised in a household that did not foster racial bigotry and intolerance of other races. Our parents had taught us that we were all God's children. Although, there were times when I thought he treated his white children better than his colored children. I was very happy being a part of the regular Army I held the rank of Sergeant in the National Guard. As such, I was placed in charge of a nine-man squad for administrative and training purposes. My training at The Infantry School (TIS) was a prelude to becoming a commissioned officer, which made completing my education of paramount importance. One of the other requirements was that I had to take a physical. During the course of the physical, I was diagnosed with heart disease, namely an intraventricular septal defect or a heart murmur. I was ordered back to Cleveland however, not until I had completed the course. Upon arrival back in Cleveland, I was given a medical discharge. I filed an appeal and refused to let this thing stand in the way of my future ambition to become a commissioned officer. After all, I had been a pilot, which required a rigid physical examination, went through basic training and showed no signs of being disabled. As a footnote, it turned out, I outlived all of the doctors who told me I would die of congested heart failure.

In my opinion, I felt that no man could out-soldier me.

During my appeal, I continued to serve with the 372nd as an unpaid volunteer. In addition, I went back to work at the Flower Shop and returned to night school and my beloved Josephine

Chapter 8

Josephine Frances Klusak was the only bright spot in my return to civilian life.

We picked up right where we left off. Along with my decision to return to school, I decided that it was time that I learned to drive a car. After all, who ever heard of a man being able to fly a plane and could not drive a car. Daddy had just bought a brand new 1952 Nash, which was shaped like and upside down boat and seats that made into a bed. Oh Boy!

A few months later, my brother, Curt bought a new car and made me a gift of his old Chevrolet. Once I began driving and had something to drive, getting around with Josephine became much easier. After many stops at the drug store and countless telephone calls, Jo and I became an item.

It was a fore drawn conclusion that every Monday, Wednesday and Friday, I would be a guest in her home. Soon, three nights per week turned into every night. I couldn't wait to see her.

During this period, I had started to work toward another goal in my life, that of being a police officer. Seemingly, many of my accomplishments were achieved by way of the back door. I.e. slipping into the army, shortcutting my pilot's license and now, being a police officer.

Through my contacts with high officials with the police department, I requested and received permission to become a special policemen or a security guard with a gun. Carrying a gun, for which I had no real purpose, was my only reason for wanting to be special. My other reason was to have an excuse to be away from Emma more than I already was.

The only money I ever made as a security guard was when I would play private detective and follow a cheating husband, like myself.

At this, I was very good. After all, I had plenty of experience at it.

One of my first cases involved a local drug store owner. I had been retained to follow him and report back to his unhappy wife of 25 years. I was given all of the necessary information and was ready to go. At the appointed time, I started to follow him from his usual place of parking. All was going very well. It was a Friday and downtown

Cleveland was starting to empty. My Chevrolet was gassed up and ready for the mission. He pulled from the parking lot with me right behind him. The surveillance was on. He preceded east on Carnegie with me following several cars behind him. Just as we were approaching the suburb of Shaker, I had moved the position of my car right behind his car. He made a sudden stop and I smacked him right in the rear. My brakes failed. I reported the incident to my client and she was more than happy because this would be one date less that he would not be able to keep.

They ultimately separated and divorced. I could have added another notch to my romantic conquest but Jo was all that I wanted.

This was my fourth year being associated with the Ohio National Guard. My appeal was still pending for official re-instatement and my love life could not have been better. Although, I looked forward to going to summer camp, I hated leaving Jo. Once each year, when we went to Camp Perry for weekend weapon's training, we could take a family member with us.

I took Josephine. We rented quarters near the camp and had a wonderful time.

Fred E. Bolden, Ph.D

I had a few good years with Josephine and then the end came. When I first met her, she worked in the factory at Richmond Brothers, a well-known men's clothing store. After she finished John Hay, she moved up the employment ladder and got a job with Eastern Airlines as a reservation clerk. It was there that she met a smooth talking con man, which happened to be white and available. She said goodbye to me and married him. I felt totally betrayed, since I had been the one to make her into the woman she had become. She dressed properly, came out of her shyness and knew how to act in almost any setting. During our last date, she was very apologetic and we even made love. She told me she would always love me, but because of the racial difference and her family and the fact that I was married, she felt her life would be better off if she married this white man. I was so devastated that I wished that I could have died right then and there, but life went on. Several more summer camps passed, as did the years of my life. It was upon my return from one of these encampments that I returned home to an empty apartment. By this time, Emma and I had been moved down to the first floor of the house. I learned that she had been seeing another man, who worked with her at the Sovereign, Hotel, now known as University Towers, a converted apartment building. I should not have blamed her, but I did. I found out where she lived and followed her but the years of my youth and infidelity, had taken their toll on the marriage. After thirteen years of she and I being together, she got a divorce. My son, Allen, chose to live with me and Orville went with Emma. After the divorce, I sort of knocked around living from place to place while mother took care of Allen.

With Josephine gone, it appeared that my link with the white female World was gone forever.

Fred E. Bolden, Ph.D

Chapter 9

A Change that would affect the rest of my life was about to unfold.

One day, while taking an inventory of fresh flowers to the May Company, which was where we had a second outlet store, I happened to look into the window of the sewing machine company, which was located right next door to the flower shop, and there sat the most beautiful woman, white or black I had ever seen in my entire life, except possibly in the movies.

As I passed her window, I gave her a gentlemanly tip of my hat and made every effort not to continue staring at her. Several days later, I went into the store, where she worked for the supposed purpose of getting change from bills to coins. I introduced myself as she opened her cash drawer and gave me change, she told me her name was Joy. During the next few days, I created reasons to visit the sewing machine company. I would go for change for the flower shop or just to pass the time of day with Mr. Gregory, the owner and enjoy being near Joy. Soon, I would time my visits so that Mr. Gregory would not be there.

It was on one of those visits that I had an opportunity to talk to her on a more personal level. We talked about her family and mine. She shared that she was married and had two children, one of whom had just been born and her name was Karen. She also stated that she was separated from her husband. Her word "separated" hung in my mind like I had to remember it on a spelling test.

It had become so that I would hurry and get my work done at the flower shop so I could take up my post watching for when Mr. Gregory would leave, so that I could at least call her. It was during one of these calls that I got up enough courage to ask her out for a date. To my great surprise, she agreed. I was totally beside myself with happiness. This just couldn't be happening to that little fat colored boy from Texas. It seemed like a million years since that same little colored boy's father had been warned to keep him away from the little white grandchild of the owner of Simpson's Boarding House.

Leatrice Joy Bond Vitantonio, who hailed from Marine City, Michigan, and liked to be called "Joy." This wonderful person God had placed in my path, was going out with me. During this time, I lived in a neat little efficiency apartment off St.Clair Avenue, on the eastside of Cleveland.

The days that followed found me floating around on the clouds. I could not have been happier.

I must have made a nuisance of myself calling her. I didn't want her to change her mind. I remember the night before I was to see her, I went home and cleaned my apartment and cleaned it again.

The floors were so highly polished that when the light was just right, you could actually see your reflection in them.

In as much as our date was to be a dinner date, I made a special trip to the Central market, a food complex in downtown Cleveland, where I had a special butcher and asked him to custom cut two of the best steaks he had. While at the market, I bought everything else to go with the dinner. I remember searching through a rack of potatoes to find the two most perfect ones in the pile.

The last time I called her, which was on the eve of our date, I recall how sultry her voice sounded and how much she reminded me of one of my favorite movie stars, Kim Novak; in fact, she looked a little like her.

On the morning of our date, Joy called me. She had a slight hesitation in her voice as she spoke. Fear gripped my heart. She spoke quietly as she told me that she would not be able to make it. My heart sank. I was mortified. It was if my body had become so desiccated that I could not swallow.

I pulled out all the stops and used all the charm I could muster, in an effort to change her mind. After much talking and almost pleading, she confided that she was afraid, mainly, because she had never dated a black man before and although she was separated from her husband, she was still married.

After much re-assuring her that people are people and other than cultural difference and color, the line between races is an overstated overblown myth. Happily, I was able to overcome her apprehensions and our date was back on.

That evening, I rushed home to prepare dinner and put any final touches on the apartment. As I reached my apartment door, I took my shoes off so as not to bring any dust into the apartment and onto my highly polished floors.

The bill of fare was to be choice cut filet mignon wrapped in smoked bacon, baked potatoes, fresh cut green beans and a fresh assortment of garden-fresh salad greens topped with homemade blue cheese along with hot garlic buttered rolls. After I had gone as far as I could, I prepared to take a shower. I carefully turned the shower on a low setting, just in case she would have called, I would hear the telephone ring. I quickly finished my shower, dried of, applied a little extra deodorant and splashed on some "old spice lotion." I dressed quickly in a casual shirt and a pair of slacks and made a quick check of the front of my building from a hallway window.

My apartment was located at the rear of the building on the third floor. At the front of the hallway, was a full window that could be raised allowing one a full view of the entire street. I perched myself in that window waiting for her arrival. She owned an old blue 1952 Ford. I made several trips back and forth to the window. Each time I would return to my apartment, I would re-check it, as if, some little gremlin had sneaked in a messed something up. After my "umptininth" trip to the window, I arrived just in time to see her little blue Ford pulling into a parking spot. I waited until she had gotten out of her car and locked it. I watched and made sure that she was just about at the apartment building and then I rushed back to my apartment, placed a pan of canned rolls in the oven, splashed on a little more old spice and started sucking on a breath mint.

I stood by the closed door of my apartment and waited to hear the sound of her clicking high heels. My heart was racing like that of a baby puppy. I positioned my hand on the doorknob and waited. The closer she came to my door, the louder the sound from her shoe heels striking the surface of the hallway's highly polished surface sounded. After, what seemed to be an eternity, the clicking heel sounds stopped and were replaced by a firm knock on my apartment door I waited a few seconds, very few, with my hand wrapped tightly around the door knob, I took several deep breathes and opened the door.

Before me stood the most beautiful woman I had ever seen in my entire life, which was the same thought I had the first time I saw her, and she was there to see me, the colored boy from Texas.

She was wearing a pair of white stretch pants with a mixed colored top. Both fitted her perfectly. She wore white high heels, which added to the lovely shape of her legs. I did my best to act reserved but pleasant. I didn't want to frighten her away on our first date. Although, I wanted to grab her and smother her with kisses, I held back. I gently grasped her hand and directed her toward the couch but she wanted to look around my apartment, which was so small that you could almost stand in the front door and see it all. She took the lead and headed toward the kitchen. She spoke in an elevated voice "something smells good." I told her dinner would be ready shortly and asked her if she wanted a drink. I made the two of us a vodka and orange juice, with mostly orange juice. Neither of us were much of a drinker at the time. She took a few sips from her glass and placed it down on the coffee table. I couldn't take my eyes off of her. She looked so beautiful. We both set on the couch and started to make small talk. She reached in her purse and took out a package of Viceroy Cigarettes. She removed a cigarette from her pack and placed it between her beautiful lightly painted lips. I had bought a table cigarette lighter so that I could light her cigarettes like they do in the movies. Although, I was not a smoker, I didn't mind her smoking at all.

We talked mostly about our families and how the times were slowly changing with respect to race relations and how she felt. One of the things that she mentioned, that I thought was refreshing, was that the reason she had never dated a black man before was because none had ever asked her out. The sound from the timer on the stove interrupted our conversation and it was time to eat. We went to the kitchen and I moved close to her so that I could direct her toward her seat at the table, but she reached for the oven door and a hot pad and removed the pan of steaming rolls from the oven. She touched one of the rolls to verify their readiness. I directed her toward her seat at the table, pulled the chair away from the table and as she seated herself, I gently nudged her chair closer to the table. I did not say the blessing nor did she seem concerned that I hadn't. I did notice that she held her knife in her right hand and her fork in the other. At first, I thought she was left handed, but she was not. She reasoned that Americans waste a lot of time changing hands from fork to knife and we should all eat as they do in Europe. I didn't care how she held her utensils, I was glad she was there.

After we had finished our meal, we went back into the living room and I held her hand as we sat on the couch. She started to take a cigarette from her pack, I quickly grabbed the cigarette lighter in preparation for lighting her cigarette. She took a cigarette from her pack and I lit it. Joy was what I would call a clean smoker. Her breath was as sweet as a baby's.

I had rigged special wiring connected to a control box next to the end of the couch so that I could control my record player and the lights without getting up form my seat. She was impressed. I had placed a record of Nat King Cole's 'Unforgettable" on the turntable. It dropped into place and soon those soft velvet tones of his flowed throughout my small apartment.

I moved closer to her and gently grasped her little hands and kissed her fingertips. I placed my arms around her slender waist as she reached her arms up around my neck. We embraced with all the sweetness and tenderness of a couple that had been in love forever.

The end of our date was signaled by her moving slightly away and announcing that it was time for her to leave. She laid her head back on the back of the couch, pulled me toward her and gave me another kiss. She rose from the couch and went toward the bathroom.

I remained on the couch in a partial daze and drifted into fantasyland. I imagined that she and I were married and at any moment, she would re-appear in a beautiful nightgown, and in a soft alluring voice invite me to come to bed. Her return to the living room shook me back to reality. I begged her to stay longer but alas, such was not to be. She reminded me that she had children and had to get back home. I did finally convince her to have just one more cigarette. This way, I was reasonably assured of one extra kiss. She took a few light puffs on her cigarette and gently pressed its burning embers out in the ashtray. She picked up the ashtray and attempted to empty it. I quickly grabbed it from her and told her I would take care of it. She placed the ashtray back on the table and started for the door, with me closely behind her. Once again, she turned toward me, with her thin lips partially parted and gave me a most passionate kiss.

I walked her down the hallway, staying as close to her as possible. We walked down the stairs and out the front door to her car. You could feel all the eyes of the street were on her. I'm certain every male on the street envied me and every female cursed her. As we reached her car, I took her keys and unlocked her door. Once again, I took her into my arms and gave her a long and passionate kiss. After she entered her car and started the motor, she rolled down the window, stuck her head out from the window with puckered lips and signaled me with her finger to give her another kiss. As we broke from that last embrace, I bade her goodbye and reminded her to drive carefully and to call me as soon as she arrived home.

I walked back to my apartment building, no; I floated back to my apartment building. I was filled with mixed feelings of pride, accomplishment and vindication, but most of all joy and happiness. My feeling of vindication was just a hold- over from my early childhood and really should have had nothing to do with her and then. Somehow, I felt that all of the indignities that I felt I had encountered in my youth and early adult life had suddenly been wiped away.

As I entered my apartment I was immediately reminded that she had been there. Her light and delicate fragrance still lingered. I found myself setting where she had sat, while holding her burned cigarettes close to my nose, hoping to recapture the sweetness of her lips.

I didn't want to move from the spot but I knew I had to wash the pots and dishes from our meal.

I rushed into the kitchen grabbed the dishes, silverware and serving bowls from the table, carried them to the sink and washed them as rapidly as I could, so that I could return to where she had spent most of her time. I stayed close to the phone. When I was not hugging the phone, I was pacing the floor like an expectant father waiting for his first-born.

I was careful not to move to far away from the telephone. I felt my very existence depended on a few strains of telephone wire. Suddenly, the phone rang. I quickly grabbed the phone and mumbled an anxious hello.

Her voice was soft, throaty and mellow. It was as if she were still in my living room. She almost whispered a hushed hello and told me that she had arrived home safely. After her greeting and it was my time to speak, I suddenly forgot everything I was going to say. My words stuck in my throat. I had gone over my speech several times, while waiting for her to call. I wanted to tell her that I had fallen totally in love with her and wanted to spend the rest of my life with her. I so desperately wanted to share with her the warmth that filled my heart. I wanted to tell her that I wanted to lock her up in my arms and never let her go. All these things I wanted to say and do, but I was afraid that I would frighten her away by coming on to strong so soon.

Our conversation was light and centered on the evening's activities. Our talk was all too brief. At the end of our conversation, I eased the phone back onto its cradle and started wishing. Wishing I had said more. Wishing she was back at my apartment. For some reason, I stayed by the phone. Maybe, I was thinking it would ring again and it would be her.

I got up and pulled my hide-away bed from the closet and got ready for bed. I sat on my couch and sorted through my phonograph records. I selected Nat King Cole's "Embraceable you" and positioned it on the turntable, turned the volume very low and slid into bed. As I positioned myself between the two fresh sheets, which I thought earlier, might be used by more than just me, I tightly locked my fingers together and placed them behind my head and started a vigil of staring at the ceiling. I recapped the entire evening in my mind. It was almost as if I were actually reliving the events of the evening.

The sweet dulcet tones of Nat's voice seemed to further etch the night into my heart. A lifetime later, I mercifully fell asleep.

Daybreak came. The sunlight slithered through the partially opened drapes and I was suddenly angry with myself for having fallen asleep. I vaulted from my bed and headed for the bathroom. As I passed my coffee table, once again my eyes became fixed on the ashtray, where the same two cigarette butts lay from the night before.

I paused briefly and mentally pinched myself and realized that the night before had not been a dream and she had actually been there.

I showered and quickly, but carefully dressed myself. I dressed as if I were going to an office, not a flower shop where I would sweep the floors, design arrangements and make deliveries. I arrived at the flower shop and hurriedly got to my work. I knew the sooner I completed the work, the sooner John, the owner, would leave. Finally, I completed the last order and John Left. He had barely cleared the front door when I raced for the telephone and quickly dialed her number.

She answered the phone on the first ring. Her voice was as sweet as it had been the night before. Once again, my mind went blank. I couldn't remember a thing I wanted to say. I blurted out that I missed her and want to see her again as soon as possible.

At that moment, someone came into her store and her voice changed to business-like.

I immediately caught on and told her I would call her later that evening.

The day went by at a snail's pace. The time to close the store finally came. I left the store hurriedly and went to my car. I drove home as quickly as I could. Upon arrival, I went directly to my couch, made my self-comfortable, picked up my telephone and dialed her number. As we spoke, I could hear a baby crying in the background. She apologized and I most certainly understood. I learned later that the crying voice was that of Karen's, her second oldest child.

We called each other frequently, however, because of her responsibilities as a single parent, our dates were few and far in between. My thoughts of her were constant. I wanted to do things for her. I wanted to share whatever I had with her.

Joy was a very proud person. She would not allow me to do anything for her, although, I had precious little myself. I did finally convince her to allow me to buy her a stereo, which I purchased from Brown Brother's furniture company, on credit, of course.

We had several more dates and each time was sweeter than the one before. Our storybook romance was not to last. After a few months, her job at the Sewing Machine company ended. Not to long after she left the company, she called me and informed me that her estranged husband had returned and she could no longer see me. She explained that her children needed their father and she would not be unfaithful to him as long as he was still in the home. She further assured me that she still loved me, these were some of the same words I had heard from Josephine years before. It was almost more than I could bear and so hard to believe that I would never see or hear from her again.

Chapter 10

Once again, my life was turned upside down. Just when I thought I had everything, it was suddenly all gone. My hopes, my dreams and my future, all gone. All that was left was a poorly taken Polaroid snap shot, a partial cartoon of Viceroy cigarettes and a comb with a few strains of her beautiful hair in it. I safeguarded and treasured those things for many years after that.

The following year I purchased a partially completed house on Land Contract. It was a nice little house located in Warrenville Township, Ohio. The contractor and owner of the house was in a hurry to sell it because the neighborhood was fast changing to black.

Shortly after buying and completing my house, I brought my son, Allen home to live with me and soon after that, Orville came to live with us.

Allen was almost fifteen when I took him by to see our new home. He wanted to move in that very same day but I told him I did not have furniture and the house had not been completed.

Over the next few months, I gathered together a few pieces of furniture, which I purchased from Brown Brother's Furniture Company.

Initially, all I had was a mattress, which I laid on the living room floor, a refrigerator and an electric stove.

I furnished one of the three bedrooms with a set of twin beds and a chest of drawers for Allen and Orville. One of the proudest times in my life was when I went to mother's and daddy's to pick Allen up to come and live with me. I enrolled him in John F. Kennedy High School, which at the time was brand new. Allen was in the first graduating class at JFK.

Toward his senior year, he started to see a young lady, by the name of Annie Shine, whom I didn't approve of but how many parents approve of their children's choice of mates.

Allen and Orville spent most of their time alone. Between the time that I spent at the Police department and the flower shop and my philandering, I was not much of a father. About the only family time we shared was on Sunday when Gerri, my Sunday girlfriend came over and cooked and cleaned the house.

Shortly after Allen graduated from JFK, he came to me with the news that Annie was pregnant. I was fit to be tied. Now, I knew how my parents felt. Her parents were all for them getting married and why not, she was pregnant.

I became rebellious and resistant, just as my father had done when I wanted to marry Emma. Like my father before, I finally went along with it. Annie's family made all of the arrangements. I eventually but reluctantly gave my official permission and did attend the wedding. I couldn't believe it; I was barely in my thirties and about to become a grandfather. This was almost as ridiculous as becoming a father at age sixteen.

After Allen married and moved into his own apartment, it was just Orville and I. My son Allen ultimately sired three sons; their names are Allen Jr., aka Rocky, who died at age 8 from Bone cancer, Antonio, aka Bunny and Pierre, who begot my two great-grandchildren, Andre' Bolden, Jr. and Quiana Marie Bolden

Orville did not want to live with me. In fact he ran away twice. He was more geared toward his mother's style of living, which was basically very unstructured and lacked direction.

Orville did very poorly in school and as soon as he was old enough, his mother allowed him to quit. Orville left the Cleveland school system illiterate, as he remains to this very day.

As I reflect back, I'm not happy with several years of my life. Prior to my sons moving in with me, my house was a typical bachelor's Mecca. Seldom would a night pass when I would not have a female guest. Unfortunately, much of this activity continued after they moved in with me.

Although, I was dating several ladies, at the time, three of them stand out in my mind as being the most impacting, one of whom was a Greek by the name of Penny, whose family owned a restaurant two doors from the flower shop. Penny was a slight built, well dressed, semi attractive middle-aged woman. She, like other previous female friends, was married, but separated from her husband. We became friends and ultimately started to date.

My relationship with Penny had no fire to it. I became friends with her five brothers, two of whom were Cleveland police officers, her sister and her wonderful mother. I was a frequent guest in Penny's mother's home.

Penny was very conscious of the color issue, almost to the point of being paranoid. I do believe that she believed that a fellow Greek was hiding behind every building and on every street corner.

On those occasions when I took her to my house, she would jump in my car and crouch down in the front seat so no one would see her with a black man. She would ride this way until we were out of the downtown area and well into the black areas.

She had a sense of style and felt that the decor in my house needed serious help.

After her marriage broke up, she had her furniture placed in storage and did not plan to use it in the future. As such, she asked me if I wanted it. Shortly thereafter, I was gifted with a house full of wonderful furniture.

I mentioned Gerri earlier, who had an interesting background. She was an ultra high priced retired call girl turned barmaid, who had, according to her, dated several movie stars. I started dating her on the nights that I did not see Penny. She would visit me on Sundays. She took it upon herself to clean and cook. She was a wonderful cook.

I managed to keep my other female friends separated by way of fabrications and careful scheduling.

My life was almost void of purpose. I was a free man with nowhere to go and no one to go there with.

I continued to go to night school and finally graduated.

You remember Josephine? Well, one day when I was taking flowers to the May Company, I spied someone that looked just like her, waiting for a bus. For just a minute, I couldn't believe my eyes. I stopped and took a better and a more prolonged look and behold, it was she.

Upon my return from the May Company, I looked up her name in the telephone book and sure enough, her name was there. I called her number and she answered the phone. I asked her about her husband and she told me that I was right when I told her that he was a con man and she was making a mistake in marrying him.

I made arrangements to see her the next night. I did not go to her home but we met by the old YMCA near downtown.

We brought each other up to date on our lives. Although, I was happy to see her, things were not quite the same. I still cared for her, but not like before. She started to visit me in my home, but not on a regular basis. I had no intention of giving up my other friends for one who had broken my heart in the past.

John, the owner of the flower shop passed away and his wife, who was getting on in years, asked me if I wanted to buy the flower shop. I had no money, but the idea of owning a business that I started to work in as a boy, intrigued me. I envisioned myself as a millionaire rising from the bottom.

My interest in the flower shop was renewed and no longer did I long to be out of the business. There were many times that I thought of my life at the flower shop and compared it to my father's life at Simpson's Boarding House. You know, almost like one of the family, but still just another nigger.

I knew that the acquisition of the flower shop would require money, but I felt it was not out of reach and with a little maneuvering and salesmanship, I could pull it off.

I had a good friend by the name of Freddy Jones, who sold furniture in a store on the opposite side of the flower shop. Freddy had a passion for colored girls. To him, black was indeed beautiful. As such, he relished our friendship.

I approached him with the idea of buying the flower shop and the idea interested him. He felt that there was money to be made.

Although, Freddy did not have any money, he had resources to acquire it. After we bought the business, with a third partner, we moved into a larger building, which was one block closer to Euclid Avenue, the main business street in downtown Cleveland.

Things went reasonably well for a while, but soon, I discovered that the old saying "All that glitters is not gold," was very true. I also found out that when you are working for someone and you began to think that if you were the boss, you could do a better job, is not always true. Things looked differently in the driver's seat.

To my utter dismay, I found no gold on East 4th Street, where the shop was located, but I did find plenty of hard work and two partners, who were not much, help. Freddy and I ultimately bought out the third partner and continued with just the two of us. After many months of trying to make a go of it, Freddy decided to move on and gave me his share of the business.

I did everything I could to promote the business, eventually, I grew weary and wanted out.

Since, over the years, I had developed many friends on the police department. Many of them were high-ranking officials, whom I kept supplied with free flowers. All of them were encouraging me to become a police officer, which I fluffed off as just another dream that would never become a reality. After all, I had this supposed heart condition and I was now an old man of 28. I could never qualify as a Cleveland Police officer.

After much prompting, I decided to give it a try. I went to City Hall and made application. Several months later, I was notified as to the date of the written examination and where to report.

The examination was held on December 12, 1960 at the Public Auditorium. The weather was cold and the place was filled with over 1500 applicants.

I knew I would not stand a chance.

I was directed to my numbered seat, whereupon I sat and waited for further instructions. I had spent many months studying the reference material, but did not feel confident. After several hours, I completed the examination and nervously handed it to one of the monitors.

It took several months before I heard from the Civil Service Commission. After many months of waiting, one day, my mother called me at the flower shop and informed that I had received a letter from the Civil Service Commission. I asked her to open it a read it to me. The notice read "We are please to inform you that you have successfully passed the Civil Service commission's examination for the position of police with a score of 83.1666%." The notice further stated that I was 272 on the list of eligible candidates. Once again, the wait was on. The days turned into weeks and the weeks into months. After a year had passed, I felt that my becoming a Cleveland Police Officer would be just another dream that would not come true.

At the time, the age limit for being a police officer was 29 and I was soon to turn 29. Wonder upon wonder happened, I was notified to report to City Hall on November 11, 1962 to be sworn in as a Cleveland Police Officer, just 41 days before my 29th birthday.

What a glorious day that was, there I stood with my hand raised, my family present and about to become a real police officer.

There were 35 in my cadet class, five of whom were black. We were issued a nightstick, a parade baton, a .38 revolver, a badge and a cap wreath. The number assigned to me was number "512."

Many times, I have often thought, that if it had not been for a very good friend, Inspector Albert Wallace, now deceased, I would never have made it. I remember on the date of my physical examination, the old heart thing came up. When the doctor told me I had a heart problem, I assured him that my supposed heart condition would in no way hamper me in the performance of my duties. I could see in his eyes that I was about to be disqualified. He told me to wait outside of his office. While waiting, I called my friend, Inspector Wallace and told him of the situation. He told me not to worry.

He called the doctor and shortly thereafter the doctor called me back in and with a stroke of the pen, my heart was OK.

You know, its sort of strange, but I have out-lived three of my police academy classmates, who were presumed healthy. I know now, more than ever, that only God knows our appointed time of death.

On Monday morning, November 13, 1962, I, along with the other cadets, reported for training at the Cleveland Police Academy, which was then housed at the 5thDistrict Police station on Chester at East 107th Street. It seemed so odd going to work at some place other than the flower shop. The Lord blessed me beyond countable measure. At last, I had a real job, which I had dreamed about since boyhood.

It didn't matter to me what I had heard about how prejudice the department was. I was now a part of it and I felt blessed to be there.

The Cleveland Police Department was very segregated during those days. If you were a black officer, you were only assigned to a predominantly black district, which was known as the 5th District.

If you were lucky, after many years on the force, a black officer could apply for the Bureau of Detectives. However, you were still restricted to work in certain districts and perform certain duties.

During my training at the academy, I was made very aware of the prejudice within the department. Most of the instructors were very racist. The fact that they were prejudice was not going to affect me. I was going to become a police officer, no matter what.

Because of the high standards of the department at the time, every effort was made to weed out anyone who was thought to be unworthy of wearing the uniform. Several of my classmates were washed out during the training, none of which were black. Unlike today, where there are affirmative action programs in place, during those days, you had to make it on your own merits. You were not appointed just because you were a female or black.

The many months spent in the academy were exciting times. I remember waking up in the middle of the night and looking at my gun and badge and being pretty proud of myself. During the time I was in the academy, several of us were given special undercover assignments, because the public would not know us. I was assigned as an undercover officer to attend Black Muslim meetings.

It had been rumored that they were currently planning an uprising. My assignment was to gather information. Their meetings were held during the evenings and on Sundays. I attended all of their meetings and made an application to join, but for some reason, I was never accepted. Maybe, they smelled a rat.

My next undercover assignment was to play the part of a "John." A John is one that frequented the various bars and places that prostitutes hung out and attempted to pick them up or better yet, have them pick you up. Arresting whores promised to be fun. As it turned out, I didn't like it. I felt sorry for them that they had to earn their living by selling their bodies.

Graduation day from the academy was another high point in my life.

The night before the ceremony, I double pressed my uniform and shined my badge until I thought I would rub the numbers off.

The day finally came. Assignments were delivered by way of Teletype.

OREO

When the Teletype started to tick, we all gathered around it like it was spurting out gold coins. I quickly spotted my name. I was assigned to the 4th District, a mixed foreign and changing to black district, which was near my home. My shift was to be from 11:00 P.M. to 7:00 A.M…In police jargon, the third sift was called the 3rd Platoon.

I was placed with an old timer, who had spent most of his years in the Detective Bureau and was very unhappy that he had been transferred out of the Bureau and back into uniform. He was a white man's nigger and working with him was pure hell.

After being on the job for a month, I made a trip downtown to visit my old friend, Inspector Al Wallace. During my visit, I thanked him for all he had done and shared with him my dislike for my partner.

He reared back in chair, looked down at me over his glasses, shoved his curved, Sherlock Holmes type pipe to one side of his mouth and started in on me. He said, "Look, you asshole, don't worry about it, you're going to be transferred tomorrow anyway." I quickly inquired as to where, but in his usual gruff manner, he said, "Never mind, you will know when the Teletype comes out."

The next day, not only were the transfers on the Teletype but I made the front page of The Cleveland Plain Dealer. "FIRST NEGRO ASSIGNED TO THE ACCIDENT INVESTIGATION UNIT OF THE CLEVELAND POLICE DEPARTMENT."

The article went on the say that my assignment had nothing to do with race. I was assigned because of my ability, which of course was a bunch of bologna. The Accident Investigation Unit was and had been, since its inception, a white only and very elite unit.

The Accident Investigation Unit (AIU) consisted of several dozen white male officers and white male supervisors. The waiting list to get into the AIU was long and went back many years. You had to have pull to get into it. Here I was one month on the job, black and being transferred into it. Within the AIU were two sub-units, The Hit Skip Squad and the Follow-up Unit, which further investigated serious and fatal motor vehicle accidents.

I was practically ostracized by all of the members, except two of them, Edward Hocevar and Paul Motiejunas, both of whom were marvelous human beings and a joy to work with. Ed enjoyed life and his family. The evidence of his family life well typified the manner in which he approached his work. He made police work fun.

Paul came from a European background however, he was very much American. I had an opportunity to socialize with his family. He sang in the Lithuanian choir. Eight hours of work went by rapidly when working with Paul. In as much as no one wanted to work with me and the fact that no openings existed on any of the district cars, I was assigned to a one-man car, which meant that I could roam the city and take any assignment. After a while, I came to enjoy working alone, which unfortunately, did not last long. One of the officers, who was assigned to the sixth District AIU car, retired. As such, I was next in line for a regular car assignment and was ultimately assigned to take his place. My partners were Russell Dunlavey and William Rayer. Between the two of them they had about 60 years on the job and thought they owned car 641, the number of the Accident Unit car. Working with them was not much fun.

The only thing one of them did was write reports and the only thing the other one did was drive. Since Willie never drove, when working with Russell, he opted to only drive when working with me.

Fred E. Bolden, Ph.D

The only good thing about working in the 6th District was it was where I had grown up.

I was unhappy working car 641, but I stuck it out and hoped for a miracle. My miracle came by way of Teletype. Some new comers were transferred into the AIU. Normally, if you were a new comer, you had to wait a long time to be assigned to a regular car. My supervisor knew I was unhappy working car 641 so; I quickly volunteered to get off the car and give it to a new comer. In fact, I gave Tommy Planinc, one of the new comers, a big hug and welcomed him to the unit.

I learned accident investigation rapidly, despite the many hurdles that were placed in my path by my fellow workers and some of the supervisors.

As time passed, one by one I began to break down my fellow worker's resentment toward me, at least on the surface.

During the time that I had been a man without a regularly assigned car, I was frequently used as a fill-in man. A fill-in man was an officer that filled in on a car when the regular man was off, ill or on furlough.

It was during those fill-in times that the men began to trust me and realized that I was a regular guy and my color would not rub off on them. Years later, after retirement, I had the pleasure of enjoying a monthly breakfast with several of my former work associates. Just to name a few, Chester Torbinski, Ralph Lest, Dan Bobby, Stanley "Stash" Wrona, Norm -"Whity"Beznoska, Eddy Rossman and Tommy Planinc. It is such a joy to meet with these wonderful guys each month and talk over old times

As time passed, I decided that it was time to continue my education. I paid a visit to Cleveland State University, which was just starting up. The old Fenn College was its base of operation.

I enrolled and started with a few basic freshmen subjects. I juggled my work schedule with my class schedules. It was shortly after my 5th year in the AIU that I became another first. I became a member of the Hit Skip Squad, which was under the command of Sergeant Ralph Lemieux, a hard working, hard-nosed guy who came up the hard way.

Ralph volunteered for the army when he was 16 and got away with it. He subsequently was part of several invasions in the European theater of operations and was singled out as one of the youngest squad leaders in combat. He never finished college but was a fierce competitor when it came to taking promotional examinations. He was probably, one of the most powerful supervisors in the department. He had a lot of influence within the department. In fact, his man was also my man, Inspector Al Wallace. In addition to his fine attributes, he was, in my opinion a bigot. However, for some reason, he liked me and I thought he was a great guy.

My partner, in the Hit Skip Unit was an officer by the name of Albert Innocenzi. Al and I took to each other like a duck to water. We were like the Peck's bad boys of the department. We were Ten-speed and brown shoes, a popular TV program, at the time about a white and black police team. He and I got along well with our sergeant. We liked him and he liked us. We got our work done and had a lot of fun doing it. Being in plain clothes, we were able to frequent many of our pleasure spots and mixed business with pleasure. Al was perhaps, one of the most A-racial persons I have ever known. Al and I would often kid each other about our choice of women. He couldn't see what I saw in white women and I couldn't understand why he liked black women.

Al will always be remembered as a great guy and a good friend.

Chapter 11

My new career as a Cleveland Police officer, along with running the flower shop and attending college, failed to slow me down, as far as my private life was concerned. I continued to see Josephine and several other friends. Josephine was now working for a Title company. Her job dealt with handling various records dealing with the filing of home deeds and mortgages and probate matters. One day, she apparently came across a name that she knew because of my past affiliation with it. She asked me if I Knew a Leatrice Joy and Nicholas Vitantonio? She told me that he had passed away and his estate was being probated. I didn't hear anything more she said after that. All I wanted to do was get to a telephone book and look up Joy's telephone number. I left the flower shop and headed for the nearest telephone booth

By the time I ran to the Euclid Arcade, where there was a bank of telephones, I was out of breath. I selected an empty phone booth, entered it and slammed the accordion door shut behind me. I quickly grabbed the hanging book and went to the V's and found Vitantonio. I searched each first name one by one. I got to the J's and there it was "joy." I reached in my pocket for a dime but did not have one. All I had was several quarters and some pennies. I attempted to deposit a quarter but dropped it. I didn't want to take time to bend down and pick it up so I took another one from my hand and deposited it. I dialed her number and the phone started to ring. After the second ring, the phone was answered. It was she. I couldn't believe that I was actually hearing her voice.

With a lump in my throat, I said…Joy; do you know who this is? She responded as if we had just spoken yesterday not several years ago. With that same soft velvet voice that I remembered so well, she said, "This is Fred Bolden." I asked her how she remembered my voice after all of these years? She said that she could never forget my voice.

Hearing her voice brought a rush of memories of almost every moment we had spent together. She told me about her husband's death and that she has wanted to call me many times but thought I might have been married and did not wish to bother me. As we spoke, just as it had been in the past, I heard a little baby crying the background. She told me she was babysitting.

We immediately made plans to see each other. I asked her if she was as beautiful as she was and she told me she had gotten fat. I told her I didn't care and very much wanted to see her.

I gave her a quick update on my life and told her that I would call her later and make arrangements to see her.

Once again, my life was about to do a flip-flop, which I believed then, as I still do, that God had a hand in it. I called her that night and made a date for Friday. She lived on the near Westside on the second floor of a house owned by her mother. Since she did not know how her mother would take to me, I told her I would pick her up at the rapid station near her home.

From the time we spoke to the day we were to meet was four days, which passed like a lingering headache. I did everything to make the days pass more quickly. I went to bed early, I cleaned clean dirt and handled additional police runs. I did my best to not see Josephine or anyone else during those four days. Time became my enemy. On the day that I was to see her, I was working the first shift and started to take off but didn't.

The house was ready. I made up a lie for Josephine so she would not come over. I was all set.

After my tour of duty, I went to the flower shop did a few things and waited for the time to close the store.

Promptly at 6 P.M., I closed the shop, rushed home, took another shower, dressed and waited. During that time I was driving a 1963 blue Cadillac, which had a built-in juice bar and an Ohio Bell radio-telephone.

I left home early for my drive to the rapid station on the Westside, where we had agreed to meet. Upon my arrival, I drove around the station parking lot and found the most ideal spot to see her when she arrived. She arrived right on the dot.

She had been driven there in a car being operated by another female, whom I later learned was her sister in law, Beverly Bond.

She spotted my car instantly, which I had described to her earlier. She moved directly toward it. She was wearing a pair of tight fitting paisley pants that yielded to every command sent them by her slim and inviting hips. I could see that she was still as beautiful as I had remembered her to be and was most certainly not fat. After I was sure that she had seen me, I got back into my car.

The lights from the parking lot were just bright enough to accent her smooth olive completion. The moon had not long begun to shine. Even in the dull glow, the soft beams from the moonlight bounced off her eyes like glitter on a lake. The closer she came to me, the faster my heartbeat became. When she was just a few feet way, she smiled, flashing her beautiful white teeth, and said "hello," I got out of my car and responded with a hi! And then gently took her by the arm and directed her toward the passenger side of my car.

We remained in the parking lot for a few minutes, while I tried to impress her with some of my car's gadgets. I had filled my portable juice bar with orange juice and vodka. I made her a little drink and it tasted awful. It was piped through rubber lines from a reservoir under the hood of the car. I filled her plastic glass and passed it to her. As I placed it in her hand, I gently kissed her fingertips. She took a sip and I could tell from the expression on her face that the drink was terrible. I apologized and took the glass from her and disposed of it. I moved close to her and our lips met with a kiss made in heaven. Her lips were soft and sweet as sugar.

As we almost broke from the kiss, I whispered to her lips how much I loved her and had missed her. She gave me a soft "Me too."

I repositioned myself behind the steering wheel of the car, turned the ignition key and started the engine. I had left the radio on, which was tuned to station WDOK, a soft music station, which at the moment was playing Tony Bennet's September Song.

I put the car in gear and slowly pulled from my parking spot and headed for the nearest exit onto Detroit Avenue. As we approached the exit of the parking lot, she opened her purse and removed a pack of cigarettes and withdrew one of them from the pack. The moment I saw her reach for the cigarette pack, I pushed the cigarette lighter into its socket and in a few seconds it popped out and I placed the glowing end to her cigarette. As she drew smoke from her cigarette, the glow from it cast a soft light on her face that made me want to stop the car and kiss her again. Not much was said as we drove to my house. After a few drags on her cigarette, she pushed it out in the ashtray. The drive home seemed long. I was in a hurry to get her there.

When we reached the house, I paused at the edge of the driveway so that she could see the freshly manicured lawn and Golden Vicarey shrubs. Her beauty paled even nature. I pressed the garage door opener's button and as the garage door opened, I kept my eyes on her the entire time. When the garage door was fully opened, I steered the car into the garage and stopped it. The moment the car was parked and the ignition turned off, I got out of the car and rushed to the passenger side to let her out. Once again, I gently took her by the arm, helped her from the car and escorted her to the side door of the house. I opened the door, which led to a small vestibule, just large enough for two people. I put my arms around her a kissed her most passionately. I helped her remove her jacket and gave her a tour of the house, starting with the rec room, which was decked out with a built-in brick bar with indirect lighting and a fancy glass back-bar. The walls were covered with highly polished oak paneling. The ceiling was of pure white acoustical tiles. The furniture was of contemporary style, right out of a Good Housekeeping magazine.

After she looked over the room, we headed for the upstairs. As we started to ascend the stairs, she turned toward me and planted another sweet kiss on my lips. I was totally beside myself and still could not believe that she was actually there.

I showed her each room. In my bedroom, I had taken the small snapshot of her from years before and had it enlarged. I had it prominently displayed on my dresser. I took the frame and removed the back, where I had placed a comb that had traces of her hair from her last visit years ago. She held the photograph in one hand and the comb in her other hand and wrapped her arms around my neck and gave me another kiss.

After we broke from our embrace, I directed her down the hallway toward the living room and invited her to sit down while I prepared our meal. I had a small 4 seater leather covered bar in my dining room, where she decide to sit, instead of in the living room.

Tucked behind the bar, I had stored a carton of Viceroy cigarettes. I presented her with the carton and she quipped, "you remembered."

The bill of fare had been planned with great care and was, of course, filled with my usual gourmet delights. The salad was a blend of tender hearts of palms, cherry tomatoes, iced celery stalks, water-gowned cucumbers, slivers of honey baked ham, Amish white cheese, pitted black olives and garnished with delicately seasoned Italian dressing.

The appetizer was clam casino, made with fresh baby clams, mixed with chopped sweet red onions, and bell peppers with pimentos simmered in garlic butter and served with a squeeze of fresh lemon.

The Entrée was Filet Mignon, wrapped in Hickory smoked bacon with an overlay of fresh snow cap mushrooms marinated in a delicately seasoned au jus.

As we set down to eat, once again, I reminded myself how much she reminded me of Kim Novak, the movie star.

I dimmed the overhead lights and lit two candles. God! Did she look beautiful!

The meal was great but I didn't want to eat, I just wanted to take her in my arms and love her. As she looked up from the table, the candlelight caused her eyes to change from hazel to green. She smiled at me and commented on how good the food was.

After dinner, we did the dishes together. I had never enjoyed doing dishes as much as I did at that moment. I washed and handed them to her for drying. She would give me a little peck on the cheek or a bump with her lovely hips. Once again, as I had done in the past, I fantasized that we were married and this was just another typical evening at home.

After we completed doing the dishes, we retired to the living room where we listened to music and danced. She danced like a professional. I felt like I had two left feet.

The evening ended all to soon. As we prepared to leave my house, she preceded me toward the kitchen door leading to the vestibule; I took her by her waist and turned her face toward mine. I kissed her several times and then lifted her from the floor and down the two steps to the vestibule landing. I took the long way back to her mother's home on West 78th Street.

During our drive, we spoke of many things. One of the things that she shared with me was that she owned a home in Brook Park, Ohio however; it was currently rented out to her sister in law Beverly's sister. All the time she was talking, I was making plans for our future a mile a minute.

At that moment, in my life, I was the happiest person in the world. Here I was, a policemen, doing what I had trained my mind and body to do since I was a boy; I was the owner of a business and had the prettiest girl in the world in love with me. She added the finishing touch to that which made my life reasonably complete.

After this joyful reunion, I called her several time per day. When I was working a one-man car, I would drive by her house and she would be waiting on the front porch with a wave and a beautiful smile. Usually, after I drove by her house, I was so happy that I had trouble giving out tickets to violators. After several weeks of dating, Joy decided that it was time for me to meet her family, which in itself, made her different than any other white girl that I had dated.

I was very uncomfortable with the idea. She assured me that it would not be a problem.

We talked it over and decided that I would casually stop over while on duty, which I thought was a good idea because they might be more willing to accept me, seeing me in my Cleveland Police uniform.

Two days later, while working a one-man car, I called her and told her I would be in the area and could stop over to meet her folks. She was very happy with the idea. I arrived at her home and parked the police car a block or so down from her home. I was mighty nervous and more than a little bit afraid. In the short time that it took me to get to her house, I managed to form in my mind many "what if's." What if they won't let me in? What if they call the Department on me?

I walked to the house, up several steps and rang the doorbell. Joy answered the door and invited me in.

The moment I entered the house, she introduced me to her mother, Mrs. Rebecca Bond. Suddenly, all of my fears and apprehensions just

Fred E. Bolden, Ph.D

melted away. The moment I met Mrs. Bond, I could tell she was from the old school and being around blacks was no big deal to her. She was elegant, matter of fact and did not put on the usual show that many white people did when they met a Negro. You know, being extra polite and overly nice, so as to cover up their real feelings or not project the wrong message. She was just like Joy. There was nothing phony about her. I liked her right away. After my first visit, I became a regular visitor.

Mrs. Bond was a rare woman. Although, from an era when mixed relationships were frowned upon and taboo, she, like Joy, fought the establishment. After a while, Mrs. Bond asked me to call her "Ma," like the rest of her children. She and I would have great conversations about the old times and black singers.

Little did I know at the time, that she had dated and been in love with a black man for many years? She had been so nice to me that I wanted to show my appreciation. I noticed in the paper that Billy Epstein, a popular black singer, was appearing in one of the downtown nightclubs. I asked her if she would like to go and see him and she quickly accepted.

She, I, Joy and Beverly Bond, Joy's sister in law, went to hear him.

I brought corsages for each of them and they were noticeably impressed. I called for them in my Cadillac. Mrs. Bond was dressed to the "nines" She wore a beautiful dress and had many diamonds on her fingers and a mink fur stole. She was a lady that radiated elegance, poise, charm and grace. The evening was a great success. I knew I had made a hit with her.

Shortly after this event, Joy moved back into her home, which was located in Brook Park, Ohio. After Joy moved, I would visit her and her children every Sunday. Her mother would be there sitting at the kitchen table smoking her cigarettes, talking and drinking coffee.

I enjoyed being around her and listening to her tales of about the good old days.

I am grateful that I had the opportunity to spend time with her before she went to be with the Lord. My father and mother, who had met her and shared my feelings about her, All to soon, after they had met and spent many wonderful hours together with her, we sadly attended her funeral. My father officiated at her funeral service and I provided the flowers.

My family was well represented. Joy's younger brother, Vance, asked his older brother, Jim, "Are only niggers going to attend Ma's funeral."

I don't believe that Jim shared those feelings, at least not openly.

I remember as Joy, Jim and I stood before Ma's casket; Jim took my arm and gently placed it around Joy's waist. Although, I was still dating Joy, I was made to feel like one of the family.

I was so proud of my Joy. She faced other members of her family, who had come from out of State, like a champ. Her attitude was if you don't like my man, you could lump it. I was her guy and she didn't care if the whole world knew it.

Joy took Ma's death very badly. Perhaps, more so than the rest of the family. Joy always felt that she had been cheated.

When they were very young children, Mrs. Bond left them and they were scattered about in various homes.

Mr. Bond, who was already deceased when I met Joy, was a ship's engineer and worked very hard at it. He was also a very heavy drinker and carouser. His alcoholism and unfaithfulness drove Ma away.

After his death, Ma decided to return and put her family back together.

Joy didn't care why her mother had left them, she was just happy that she had come back to her.

I will always believe that Joy's strong sense of family loyalty was because of her early childhood.

Someone once said, "If something can go wrong it will," well, I believe it.

My heaven on earth was about to be disrupted once again. No matter what troubles Joy and her deceased husband had, his death was devastating. There she was with four young children, one an infant with no father or husband.

One day she called me and told me that she had to see me. I rushed right over. When I arrived, I noticed that she was not her usual bubbly self. I asked her what was wrong? She took a deep breath and told me what she had gone through after her husband had died. One of his so-called friends had come to her rescue and was a great help. The long and short of the whole thing was she had married this man after Nick died. She dubbed him "Asshole." His real name was Johnny D. Although her marriage to him only lasted eight days, she did marry him and now he wanted her to come back. He had bought a home in Vermilion on the Lake.

Joy had convinced herself that because of the girls and maybe the color issue, it might be best.

Obviously, her decision did not set well with me. We said our good-byes and she and the children packed up and moved. She was only there a short while when she realized that this guy was truly an "asshole" and she had made another mistake. She, along with the help of her sister in law, packed up and moved back to Cleveland.

Shortly after she returned to Cleveland, she contacted me and wanted to get back together. I gladly consented.

For the next year we dated and all was good. We had a regular routine. She would visit me during the week and I would spend every Sunday with her and the kids, which I truly loved. I always came loaded with bags of goodies. The kids would mob me as soon as I hit the door, which I looked forward too. As time passed, I looked forward to seeing the kids almost as much as I did joy.

Sundays were filled with fun and games. The only bad part about Sunday was when it was time for me to leave. Joy made it perfectly clear that I could never spend the night at her home with the kids, which I understood.

My Sunday girlfriend, Gerri, used to wait for me to come home and be with her. As time went on, I didn't care if she waited or not. After several weeks of this kind of treatment, she took the hint and found herself someone else.

Realizing that Joy was a person of strong convictions, especially concerning family and moral values, I could tell that it was time for me to make some sort of move toward a permanent relationship.

One Thursday, while Joy was visiting me, I asked her to marry me.

When she said yes, I became suddenly afraid; I didn't really think that she would accept my proposal

The following day, I went to my friend Bill, who owned Forrest City Jewelry, and asked him to design a set of rings for her.

I was so anxious, I wanted him to make the rings while I was there. He laughed and said "sure, right away." He was joking, but I wasn't.

Two weeks later he called me and asked me to come to his shop to pick up the rings. The rings were beautiful. Bill was a very nice guy.

Unfortunately, a few weeks later, he was found murdered in his shop. It was discovered through investigation that he was heavily involved with prostitutes and was robbed and murdered by one of them and her pimp.

I wanted the time and place to be just right when I presented the rings to my Joy. I called and made reservations at the Keg & Quarter for Saturday night. When Saturday arrived, I went and picked her up. She looked gorgeous. While on the way, I reached over to pat her leg and she suddenly opened her legs and exclaimed, "I don't mind you feeling my legs, but I don't want you to snag my stockings." At that moment and because of her remark, I wanted to take her to a hotel and make love to her.

As we pulled up in front of the Keg & Quarter entrance, the valet was waiting to open the door of the car. When I reached her side of the car, she looked up at me and flashed a smile that had become most familiar to me.

As we reached the main dining room, the Matre'd approached us and greeted us by name.

Joy was impressed. After we had been seated, our waiter presented himself to us. He too, greeted us by name and placed two cocktails in front of us compliments of the owner, Jim Swingos.

I hurriedly took a sip from my glass and placed it back on the table. I must have been looking at her strangely because she asked me what was wrong? I asked her to close her eyes and give me her left hand. As she placed her hand in mine, I slipped the engagement ring on her finger. Her eyes popped open, she grinned and leaned over and gave me a long and wonderfully wet kiss.

The Snapshots, the name of the band that was appearing that night, caught the cue and made a public announcement. They played a special song for us and we got up and danced.

Although, I was not much of a dancer, she made me look like Fred Astair.

After the announcement, drinks started to come to our table from all of our friends that were there that night. My best friend Al kept us supplied with drinks all night. Joy looked even more beautiful as the evening wore on. I wanted to show her off as one would a beauty queen.

I wanted to impress her further. I knew she had not been to many places, so I told her I was going to take her on a cruise to celebrate our engagement. She was very excited about the idea. I looked forward to being alone with her for more than just a few hours.

I booked passage for us on the S.S. Sunward, a liner out of Norway, sailing from Orlando Florida. This ship was staffed by mostly Jamaicans, which meant that the food would be different and very good.

On the date of our departure, I drove to her house to pick her up, which in itself gave me much joy. Even the kids were excited for us. There were numerous requests from the kids to bring them back a gift.

We flew to Orlando where we boarded this beautiful ship. It took us overnight to get to the Bahamas. We dined, drank, danced, slept, dined, danced, slept and had non stop fun all the way to the Bahamas

During our trip, there was an incident, which we laughed about for years after. Because of my diet or whatever, I knew my poop was less than aromatic, as such, I took along a can of air freshener to use whenever I went to the toilet, which I carefully hid behind the toilet bowl. Each time I pooped, I would pull out my little can and give the room a little spray. My Joy told her sister in law that my crap smelled just like pine.

The next morning we arrived at our port of call. We had previously elected to have the first sitting for our meals, which meant we ate early. We quickly ate our breakfast and prepared to disembark from the ship.

In as much as I had made the trip before, I took the lead and laid out our plans for the day. Bay Street, the main street in Nassau, is located in the heart of downtown and right next to the docks where all the ships came in. Although, I had seen Bay Street many times, it always held a sort of magical attraction for me, with its many straw marketers and hucksters lining the street and storefronts.

I would not allow her to buy anything the first day because the prices were always lower on the day the ships left. Although, I thought I was a pretty savvy shopper, Joy was better at it than I.

We toured the island, which meant going to every shop and stopping at every sidewalk merchant's stand down Bay Street and up Queen Street, which was the second busiest main street. We strolled, took pictures and looked. One of the pictures we took was with a little native girl that Joy had taken a liking to. For a hot minute, I thought Joy was going to take this little pigtail hair girl back home with us.

Our first night in port meant dressing up and sampling some of the local nightlife. Just when I thought Joy could not get lovelier, when she completed dressing, she totally took my breath away. We took a Limousine to the Paradise Hotel and Casino, the swankiest place on the island, at the time.

Joy wore a pink evening gown and a borrowed mink cape. She was by far, the prettiest woman in the casino. I played the dice tables, which I knew nothing about and Joy played the slot machines. After we had our fill of the casino, we went to the Emerald Beach Hotel. The tourist there were loud and having a lot of fun. The waiters and waitresses were native and danced with their serving trays on their heads. We danced the native dances and had one jolly good time. We spent three wonderful days in Nassau, which passed all to quickly.

Our last morning in port was spent going back to some of the shops for gifts. We walked Bay Street from one end to the other. My Joy touched everything at every shop. By the time were through, I was sick and tired of Bay Street and wanted to get back on the ship.

We finally returned to the ship and stored our cache of goods and prepared for the Captain's Ball.

Once again, I saw a person of rare beauty. Joy dressed in another beautiful evening gown that would have done any fashion model proud. She looked almost too beautiful to touch. Because of Joy's complexion, she required little or no makeup. When I went to kiss her, she drew away and asked me not to mess up her lipstick.

She saw the hunger in my eyes and drew me close to her and gave me a most passionate kiss. After that kiss, I didn't want to leave our cabin.

The Captain's Ball was the highlight of the cruise. Every passenger had to dress in formal attire. Upon entering the main ballroom, the captain greeted you and a photograph was taken with him. I felt ten feet tall standing next to Joy. She held onto my arm with the grace of a queen.

After the ball was over, we went to the top deck, where there was a small intimate nightclub called the Crow's nest. We sipped on a couple of native drinks and recapped the events of the day and made plans for the future. We walked the moon light bathe deck arm in arm. Neither of us could believe that our trip was about to end.

Early the next morning our ship pulled away from the dock to the tune of "Yellow Bird," being played by a native steel drum band. It was a sad time for us as well as for the others aboard. The return trip home was much faster than the trip over, or at least it seemed that way.

When we arrived home, the children were waiting with wide eyes and open arms. I don't know, but I think, it was then that I realized how much I really loved the children. My love was truly like unto that of a maternal father. Life pretty much picked up where we left it before our trip. Two weeks later, my fiancée called me and informed me that she didn't believe in long engagements and that she could not preach one thing to the girls and do something different herself. I was told in no uncertain terms that I was going to have to "dodo" or get off the pot.

She accepted that I had been a bachelor for the last thirteen years and the idea of marriage had to sink in, but it had better not take to long.

I must admit that I had figured on a long and pleasurable elimination of all of my female playmates and then think about a wedding date.

I remember one evening, during this elimination period, Josephine was visiting me and the phone rang, it was Joy. I made a vain attempt to sound like I had been sleeping but glad to hear from her. We traded a few words and I tried to get her off of the phone, but she persisted on talking. She informed me that she was out and was going to take a ride by my house. I attempted to dissuade her because of the late hour and thought that I had been successful, but a few minutes later, the phone rang again and it was she.

This time, in a very stern voice, she informed me that she was in my neighborhood and if anybody was in my house other than me, I had better get rid of her because she was on her way over. I quickly aroused Josephine and told her of the situation and asked her to get dressed and leave, which she did.

A short time later, Joy arrived. I could tell the way she got out of her car that she was more than a little bit upset. As she walked toward me, I could sense that it was all over. I stood by my side door and as she got to the door, she pushed me aside and walked directly to the bedroom and then returned to the kitchen.

I tried to explain away this very embarrassing situation, but there was really no way to explain it.

I reminded her of the many time she had left me because of her situations, but as she pointed out, she was honest about those situations and we were not engaged at the time. This was my first opportunity to be on the receiving end of Joy's innate ability to tell a person off in such a way that you were stripped of all of your defenses and for the most part, she did it without vulgarity. She told me that she loved me but she would not put up with any "shit."

By the time the dust settled, I promised her that I would divest myself of all of my girlfriends and make definite plans for our wedding.

As daybreak was about to loom, she rose from her seat and prepared to leave. I walked her to her car and her last words to me were "Get rid of them now or else!"

The following Monday, I called my next-door neighbor, who was a realtor, and asked him to put my house up for sale. I called Annie, Allen's wife and asked her to help me pack. I gave them much of my furniture and prepared the rest for trucking to Joy's house.

The next few weeks were hectic but exciting. I contacted my old school chum, Dr. Hyman Stockfish and made an appointment with him for us to take our blood tests. A few days later, I picked Joy up and we went to Hy's office and had our blood drawn. Several days later, he called a told me the results were back and I could pick up the paper work. I called Joy and she agreed to go with me to pick it up. After we picked it up, we went and applied for our license the same day. I still couldn't believe that I was going to get married again.

I began to spread the word throughout my police unit about my upcoming marriage. Most of my white co-workers offered me words of advice such as; we will have lots of problems, the world is not ready for such marriages etc. I must admit that there was considerable consternation on my part, not because of the color issue; I felt that I might lack the moral fiber to make an honest commitment. No matter, it was to late to change my mind now, plus, I was madly in love with her and the children. If history has a place for us little nobodies, my Joy deserves to be mentioned under the G's for guts. Here she was a beautiful young white widow, with four very young white female children, living in an all white neighborhood, about to marry a black man from the eastside.

Most of her children took to the idea. I say most, not all. Little Leatrice Joy cried and begged her mother not to get married or at least wait for another year. To this day, I don't know the significance of

Fred E. Bolden, Ph.D

one year, but as it turned out, from engagement to marriage, it was a year. Joy and I joked about Leatrice, because she was the darkest of all our children. Joy used to say, "That one is really yours." I would come back with they are all really mine.

When Joy broke off with me the first time, she became pregnant right away with Leatrice. In as much as we had been intimate, the possibility was there.

Chapter 12

At last our wedding day arrived, March 5, 1971 and I was as ready as I was ever going to be. I bought a new suit, new shoes and a toupee, which Joy hated. The wedding ceremony took place in the same house, as had my first wedding, some 26 years before. Daddy performed the service and was happy to be doing it. I remember thinking, how different this wedding was. Both my mother and father were very pleased with Joy. My mother said that Joy was the best thing that could have ever happen to me.

In attendance at the wedding was my friend Al, who acted as best man, a few friends from the police department, Joy's brother, Jim and a few of my family friends. Joy and I both wished that Mrs. Bond could have been there.

After the wedding ceremony, we had some light refreshments and drove to the Keg & Quarter. We didn't stay long at the Keg & Quarter.

As Joy and I drove home, we held hands and would kiss at some of the stoplights. I still couldn't believe that I was married. When we arrived home, Sherry, our oldest daughter, was still up and was the first one to greet us. Joy yelled out "Well, its legal now."

I felt strange sleeping with her in her bed with the children there. I used to wake up and think that it was time for me to go home.

Our honeymoon was delayed for one month so that it would coincide with my furlough from the Police Department. For the next few weeks, I went about the business of adapting to being a new husband and father.

We began to make plans for our honeymoon. Alice Lee, our next-door neighbor, was asked to baby-sit our children, to which she gladly consented. When the big day arrived, we drove to the airport, parked my car in the police parking lot, boarded our plane and headed for Las Vegas.

The big jumbo jet made good time, taking us to the land of glitter and gold. When our plane touched down in Vegas, the only thing I thought of was for the first time in along time, I didn't have to lie to anyone about where I was going or with whom. It felt good.

Joy held onto my arm as we walked toward the baggage claim area. She looked up at me like I was the only person in the world.

Joy was from the old school. She believed in holding onto the arm of her male escort, white gloves and hats.

Our luggage was one of the first to appear on the luggage carousel. I quickly retrieved it. My brother, Curt, who lived in Vegas at the time, met us and helped with our luggage. He directed us toward the parking area where he had parked his vehicle. Curt drove us to the Sand's Hotel, where I had gotten us a package deal for honeymooners. Our room was lovely. It had a dressing room and a separate living room. We had our own balcony overlooking the swimming pool. Our room was everything any newly weds could have wanted. Our first night in Vegas was spent with my brother, Curt. He met us at the hotel and took us sight seeing. He had dinner with us and saw a couple of shows. He also bugged me about gambling. My bride saw that I was being annoyed, so she took my brother in hand and directed him away from where I was playing.

Joy played the slot machines and once again, as I had in the Bahamas, I rolled the bones. Our first evening did not end until the wee hours of the morning and by that time we were very glad to see our bed.

I think I was out the minute my head hit the pillow. You would think that sleep would have been the last thing on my mind, being on my honeymoon and all, but sleep I did. To add insult to injury, I did the same thing the next night.

My Joy cried and bitterly complained about my lack of amourousity and I explained that I was having so much fun being with her that sex was in the back of my mind. Joy didn't buy that. I figured I had better cut the mustard or I would be in divorce court before I was married good.

When our honeymoon ended, Joy said she had enjoyed herself, but I knew she was disappointed that we had not made love more than we had.

On the morning that we were to leave, I went down to the casino to give the dice table one more chance to make good. It was a good thing that I did. I won enough money in that short period of time to pay for our trip. We purchased souvenirs for the kids and headed back to good old Brook Park, Ohio.

I rapidly adapted to the role of father and husband. Believe it or not, I enjoyed it. The kids were great fun to be around. For a while, they called me Fred, then one day, Karen, our second oldest child, called me "pop" and from then on, the other kids just sort of fell in line and followed suit. From that day to this, I have been Pop, Daddy or Dad.

For some reason, the term stepfather or stepdaughters was never used in our home. I never considered myself a stepfather. To this very day, it seems strange when I hear someone refer to my children as my "stepchildren." I usually correct them and say, do you mean my daughters?

I remember the day I went to the Cleveland Police Department and initiated the necessary paper work to add my new family to my hospital insurance plan. I felt as proud as punch. My children filled my heart with joy. The lady at City Hall, where I had to go to complete the forms, commented that I was very lucky to have four girls. I agreed with her then, as I do now. A man is blessed when he has daughters.

Everything seemed so automatic; as if a script had been written for a play and each of the actors were playing their roles to perfection. My daughters and I did our share of horse playing and house tussling.

Each day, as they prepared for school, I laid out their lunch money and yelled at them when they did not listen to their mother. It took so little to make my children happy.

One day, I brought home a giant flower box, the type that the wholesale flowers came packed, all wrapped in silver foil paper. Inside the box, I had tucked a huge stuffed dog, which was for my little Rebecca's fourth birthday. When she spied the box and was told it was for her, her little eyes grew to the size of quarters. She started waiving her arms around in a wild frenzy. She tore into the box, took out the big dog, which was as large as was she, and gave it a big hug. She ran to me and gave me an equally big hug and a kiss, which totally wiped me out.

I recall the day I took Becks to meet my mother, whom she had never seen before. As we went up the stairs, which led to mother's house, she held two of my fingers tightly in her little hand. I knocked on mother's door and she yelled out "whose there?" I yelled back, its me mother. Mother opened the door and greeted us with the kind of smile that only a mother and grandmother could give. As we entered the house by way of mother's kitchen, with its old style wooden cabinets, porcelain sink and linoleum covered floor, my mind flashed back to the many times I had enjoyed one of mother's fine cooked meals.

Mother motioned for us to come in. She smiled at Becks and reached down for her to come to her but Becks quickly withdrew and grabbed me around the leg and hung on for dear life.

My mother must have seemed strange to her, since she had never been around black women before. After I assured her that it was alright, she cautiously placed her little hand in the outstretched hands of my mother's, but as soon as she could, she returned to her place of familiar safety, wrapped snugly around her daddy's leg.

The novelty of my having a white wife soon wore off around the police station and Joy was referred to the same as the other wives, "The ole lady." Life was everything I wanted it to be. I had a beautiful wife, good health, a fine house, four lovely children and a good job. It was a pleasure to go to work, even when I would be called out in the wee hours of the morning for a special assignment.

Fred E. Bolden, Ph.D

No matter what shift I was working, I always got to work early so that I could stand around the coffee pot and gossip.

Most people think that all police work is about chasing speeders, shooting people and kicking down doors, such is far from the truth. Although, we do those things, police work can be very boring, not at all like you see on television. I thank God that I never had to shoot anyone. In fact, I hate guns. The only time I had to be disciplined during my career was for not attending regular firearms practice.

I enjoyed being a policeman. I was blessed to have had a boyhood dream come true. The 24 years I spent with the Cleveland Police Department were perhaps the happiest of my life. The guys I worked with and the various experiences I had will always be remembered.

This little reflection on my police history would not be complete unless I mentioned my old friend and partner, Ernie Hayes.

Ernie hailed from the southern part of Ohio and was truly one of the good old boys with a modern twist. We rode around the city looking for suspect hit skip vehicles. Ernie was a true professional in accident reconstruction, perhaps, one of the finest in the State. On the humorous side, Ernie, had a propensity for emitting crackling sounds caused by escaping gas from his rectum. Aside from our shared joviality, I learned a lot from Ernie. He was the most knowledgeable accident investigator I had ever worked with. When Ernie transferred from The Accident Unit to the bureau, it saddened me. One day we met in the elevator and he shared with me that he was not too happy with one of his partners.

I asked him why not? His reply was that the man was all right but he just couldn't appreciate a good fart. Once in a while I still see my friend, Ernie. In fact, if I had to identify a truly good friend from the department, Ernie would be on the short list.

Joy was proud to be the wife of a Cleveland Police officer. She made the fact known to all who knew her. Whenever an article appeared in the paper about me she would cut it out and place it in our scrapbook. She tapped any news items from TV that involved my work and me.

It's hard to remember my life without Joy and my children. Its like I have had them all of my life. Even now, as I walk through the house and see certain things, they bring back memories of days gone by when fun and laughter filled every part of the house.

I can still hear Joy yelling from the front door of the house for the children to come home from playing when it was time for dinner.

Somehow, when I yelled, they never heard me, but when she yelled, they came from all directions.

Although, everyday was a fun day, Christmas was perhaps the best of all. Joy, along with her best buddy and sister in law, Beverly Bond, spent days and weeks shopping. They went from Brook Park to Akron, Ohio. What a team the two of them made. They were two of the most unlikely pair you could imagine, other than their similar childhood experiences of abuse. Beverly's divorced mother, who could not care for her, her brother and sister, placed Beverly in an orphanage during her early pre-adolescent years.

Beverly didn't fare to well in the orphanage. In fact, she was thrown out of the home for fighting, which tells you a little about Bev's makeup. One day, while visiting Beverly, who now lived several streets over from our home, I was kidding her about saying "shit" so much. She said she had been saying shit since she was two years old and was not about to stop saying it now.

Over the years of my marriage, because of the close relationship between my wife and Beverly, I came to resent her. When I looked for a reason to excuse my errant behavior, in the area of extracurricular activities, I would often use the excuse that it was because she spent so much time with Beverly. I eventually came to accept the pecking order. First came the children, then Aunt Beverly and uncle Jim and then me.

At times, when we argued, I reminded her of the time she spent with Beverly and how, although she spent a lot with her, Beverly never neglected her man. Although, I used this as an argument to excuse my conduct, I knew, even then, that I was wrong. I still, to this day, regret the lost time not spent with Joy and my children.

Fred E. Bolden, Ph.D

Chapter 13

My first official Christmas as husband and father, was very exciting. The house was filled with sounds of laughter, screaming kids and conversation so loud that it would blow the needle off the face of a decibel meter. All of this activity was in concert with the rattle of pots and pans, being used to prepare all kinds of food for the holiday. Joy made lasagna, which was the best; there were trays loaded with various lunchmeats and cheeses, cookies and baked goods of every description.

The living room furniture was re-arranged so as to accommodate the giant Douglas fir tree, which my wife and Beverly had picked out.

I went with her once. It turned out to be a most exasperating experience.

My wife would spend scandalous amounts of time looking over every Douglas fir tree on the lot. Make no mistake, no tree would ever grace our living room unless it had personally spoken to my wife and assured her that it was the right tree for our house.

Decorating the tree was a family project, which lasted well into the night, but when completed, our tree was the prettiest one in all of Brook Park. After my wife had completed putting the finishing touches on the tree, she would slump in her favorite chair, light up a cigarette and sip on a cup of cold coffee.

As the lights from the tree would flicker on and off, I could see their reflection in the tired eyes of my bride, who although exhausted, would periodically jump up from her seat and move an ornament or a light or slightly turn the tree.

Her favorite ornament, not made by one of our children, was an old gunnysack and cardboard angel, which she had had for many years.

After countless moves, tugs and changes, I said to my bride, Honey, let's go to bed.

She carefully pushed the glowing embers of her cigarette against an ashtray, rose from her seat and moved toward the steps, with me right behind her. As she reached the bottom steps, I gave her a little pat on her behind, which she shook at me as she turned and gave me a little kiss, the sweetness of which, I still remember.

To this day, I have never been able to pick out a tree quite like the ones she and Beverly used to bring home. Their trees were shaped better, stayed fresh longer and smelled better.

Christmas morning started with pandemonium and rose from there.

Although, I had already been exposed to loud talking and yelling, I quickly learned that such sounds were a norm for our home.

Recollection of that first Christmas still warms my heart and gives me a storehouse of memories to draw from. I can still see the faces of my beautiful daughters as each of them tore into their gift wrapped packages. The echo of their voices still rings in the recesses of my heart.

Two years after we were married, my wife came to me with a bit of news that just about knocked me off of my feet. It was Sunday morning and I was still in bed. Joy was in the process of getting dressed. She turned toward me and said, "Honey, I missed my period this month." I replied that she should not worry it would come. She just smiled and said, "Honey, this chick knows when she is pregnant, and I am pregnant." I jumped out of bed and put my arms around her and asked her if she was sure? She responded with "Yep."

Many thoughts ran through my mind. Such as, I'm too old to have another child. How would the girls take to another child in the family? Will we be able to afford another child?

When my wife looked me in the eyes and told me how much she loved me, everything was great and we started to make plans for the new comer.

As the weeks and months passed, she grew bigger and bigger and if possible, more beautiful than ever. There was a sort of glow about her. I was so proud whenever we went somewhere together.

On august 23, 1973, her water broke. I rushed her to the hospital, where she was taken immediately to the delivery room. I took my position, along with the other expectant fathers and waited, waited and waited. I took a chair and drifted off to sleep. During the wee hours of August 24, 1973, I was awaken by the gentle voice of a nurse telling me that my wife had delivered a healthy baby boy and wanted to see me.

I ran ahead of the nurse with her guiding me in the direction of the delivery room of Southwest Berea Hospital.

When we arrived at Joy's room, there she was holding a little bundle close to her chest. There he was Fred Earl Bolden, II. She yelled to me "Honey, honey, I've got me a son." I was numb with joy, not just because of our baby, but because of how happy my wife was. In the years to come, she shared with me that her pregnancy with our son, was the happiest pregnancy she had ever had.

After Freddy was born, Joy remained in the hospital for several days to have a tubaligation performed. There was little doubt in either of our minds that if she had not had that tubaligation, we would have had a new baby every year.

Although, I was now 42 years old, I had very little experience changing diapers and washing poop out in the toilet, I soon got the knack of it. To my surprise, I didn't mind it at all. I suppose my reason for not minding it was that I loved that little guy so much that I never got tired of being near him. When Allen and Orvile were infants, I would change a diaper with a little pee on it, but that was where I drew the line.

Just as my four daughters had brought joy into my life, my infant son was a gift from heaven. Each day after work, I couldn't wait to get home and hold him.

One of my fondest memories of him as he grew was when he would climb up on the arm of my chair so that he could kiss me when

I came home. As the years passed and my children grew older, we became involved in camping. I got the bright idea to form a camping club made up of police officers and their families.

I assembled some 75 officers and held a meeting. Unfortunately there was not enough interest. As such, I opened it up to include civilians. I wound up with sixty-one families and raised $10,000, which represented the down payment on a campground in West Salem, Ohio. We named the campgrounds, "Smokey Haven Campgrounds."

Owning our own campground was very exciting. The family took to it very well Joy and I talked it over and decided to buy a trailer. We shared our idea with a former neighbor of ours, who owned a mobile home business in Pennsylvania and asked him if he could get us a good deal. We looked at several trailers and finally decided on a little 24-footer, which was big to us, since it slept 8 people.

My wife and I drove to Pennsylvania in an Oldsmobile, which we had bought from Vance, my brother in law. Neither Joy nor I had ever pulled a trailer before, let alone pulled one up and down the mountainsides of Pennsylvania, but we did it.

Fred E. Bolden, Ph.D

The first few weeks that we owned our trailer, we parked it in our driveway. In as much as I had no experience in backing up a trailer, we called Vance, who was a professional truck driver, to back it in for us. Joy and I and the kids, would just go in the trailer and sit. We were all very happy and looked forward to our first trip.

The first time we pulled our trailer on a trip was to Clay's Park, where an annual fair was being held. It was at Clay's Park where little Freddy received his first injury.

A big, but friendly Shepherd dog jumped up on him and clawed his beautiful little cheek, which required two stitches to close.

When I took Freddy to the nearest hospital, it just about broke my heart when he was taken from my arms into surgery. His little voice was screaming out to me "Daddy, daddy, come with me, come with me." He was finally strapped into a papoose and the slit in his cheek was sewn closed.

Freddy's unhappy frolic with the dog was not to end our weekend emergencies. Not an hour later, little Joy Marie fell into our campfire and had to be rushed to the same hospital where we had just returned with Freddy. Fortunately, her hands were not badly burned. On the way to the hospital, we kept them sticking out of the window to keep them cool.

Finally, the day came when we pulled our trailer to Smokey Haven Campgrounds. I was a bit apprehensive. I hoped I could pull it to the campgrounds. I thought, hey, I pulled it from Pennsylvania, pulling it 50 miles on flat highways would be nothing. I backed our car up to the trailer and hitched it up as though I had been doing it for years. We topped off our water supply and I was ready to travel. Joy yelled out a few more commands to the girls and soon we all piled into the car and off we went. Although, the hour was growing late and I didn't want to pull at night, when we were about half way to the campgrounds, we stopped at a truck stop. I felt like a big time truck driver as I pulled our rig into a parking slot reserved for vehicles with trailers.

Thank God, it was a spot that did not require us to back out. After we had enjoyed our hamburgers and fries, we were once again on our way.

It was well into dusk when we arrived at the campgrounds.

As we pulled in, our first sight was that of a high grassy knoll, which made a most fitting backdrop for the winding roadway leading into the campgrounds. There was still a slight remnant of the sun's rays behind the grassy knoll, which later became known as the Indian Hill. It was legend that the hill had treasure buried in it.

As we approached our temporary site, there was a small group of campers holding up a sign that read "Welcome Mr. President."

Our first weekend at the campgrounds saw all 61 families present. The next few weeks were spent getting our campsite ready to pull our trailer onto it. We chopped trees, poured cement and laid water lines and sewage pipe. I often wonder who has that little trailer now, but if it could talk, it would share many wonderful memories of our happy family.

One special memory for me was when my son, Freddy first pooped in a toilet. I remember the day Joy was trying to get him to sit on the toilet seat, but he just wouldn't go. I came in a remarked that the reason he could not go was because he needed a little privacy. After all, we were all standing around him waiting for him to drop his first pooper in the toilet. With that, we closed the toilet door and shortly thereafter, we heard a jubilant cry from the toilet. It was Freddy yelling, "I did it, I did it, I pooped in the toilet."

Joy and I looked in the toilet bowl and lo and behold, there in its watery depth, appeared several deposits of reprocessed hotdogs and beans. Thus came the potty training of my wonderful son.

Our weekends at Smokey Haven were wonderful. My wife complained about the extra work, the older children complained about nothing and I complained about all the responsibilities placed on the president of the campgrounds. As the children grew older, we allowed them to stay home and work and we would take Rebecca and Freddy with us. Most of the time, this would not set well with Joy, because she knew the older girls were acting up at home, without us being there. As the family grew older, we, or I should say I, felt we needed a larger trailer.

I convinced Joy to buy a new 39-foot Coachman trailer. It was a beauty. It did everything but talk. We sold our smaller trailer and moved in our new one. Joy began to loose interest in coming out as often as she had in the past. When Jim and Bev became caretakers and permanent residents, her campground interests became renewed.

My brother in law, Jim, was a good caretaker. He could repair most things and was generally liked by most of the campers.

Fred E. Bolden, Ph.D

I enjoyed being around Jim. He had a talent for relating historical events as though he had actually been there. He would have made a great history teacher. Over the years, bickering, jealousy and a need for power, by certain factions, resulted in me and my family moving away from Smokey Haven Campgrounds.

My wife had seen certain problems coming long before we left the campgrounds. She warned me but I was hardheaded and too trusting. The source of our problems was the son in law of the previous owners, who aspired to own the entire campgrounds. To my undoing, I felt that I had a friend in this young man. Joy saw him as being a backstabbing drunk. As time went on, he obtained a majority of the campground stock and I sold him ours and we moved on.

Camping was not yet out of my blood so I went shopping for another piece of property. I called my buddy Ernie and told him of my plans and what I was looking for. Ernie invited me down to Southern Ohio, where he was raised and had since returned there after his retirement from the police department.

We looked at 21 acres of woods and I saw a vision. Unfortunately, my wife did not see the same vision. Over the strong objections of my wife, I plunged in and bought the land and started to develop it into a campground.

I hooked up with a local good ole' boy who had several pieces of excavating equipment. Before you could say, let's go camping; I had put him and his bulldozer to work. He plowed in a half a mile of roadways and dug two lakes. The phone company laid telephone lines, we had a well dug and we strung electric lines. Walla, Bolden's Acres was born. I was as happy as a pig in swill.

My wife was not so happy, but she liked what had been accomplished.

Our new land was heavily wooded and was located 33 miles north of Wheeling West, Virginia. A few weeks later, I returned to Smokey Haven Campgrounds and had our mobile home towed to Bolden's Acres.

Life at Bolden's Acres was not as much fun as it was at the old campgrounds. The girls were all grown up and Freddy was fast growing up. I bought trailers for each of the children, who now had children of their own. No matter how hard we tried to accept our new campground, it was just not the same. It was not as pretty and it was 135 miles from home. It was just not Smokey Heaven.

Fred E. Bolden, Ph.D

Although, we were a happy family, our lives were constantly changing. The flower shop was going down hill fast and the end was in sight.

Another business opportunity came my way, in the form of a poultry stand, which was located inside of the Jupiter store, which was a part of S.S. Kresgee's. Once again, I found myself talking to my wife about another venture and once again, she didn't like the idea, but went along with me.

We bought the stand and completely changed it. We put in cooked items, which my dad prepared. He was happy to be working again.

This little stand took off like wildfire. It became a soul food Mecca, the first in downtown Cleveland.

We gave jobs to all of our children and some of their friends, one of which turned out to have very light fingers. It was comical how we discovered her thieving ways. One day, one of her children made the statement, "Mother the only thing you bring home is chicken, we are tired of chicken."

Our little food stand was doing so well that Burger King looked it over and before we knew what had happened, they bought the building and we were out in the cold. We moved to Kresgee's other store, closer to Public Square, but it was far from the success we had enjoyed at Jupiter. We ultimately closed it down and bought a bar.

We took in a partner, who knew the bar business. It became clear, after a few months that the bar could not support two families.

My life was indeed full. I was operating a business and going to college. My dear wife begged me to get out of business and just be a policeman, but the Bolden curse of having thick heads, wouldn't allow it. A year into the bar business, my partner became involved in an altercation, which resulted in his arrest, which prohibited him from being a part of the business any longer. My wife and I took over and totally changed the type of business. We added dancing girls and a full food menu. My daughter, Sherry was our barmaid and we became so busy that she couldn't pour the booze fast enough.

I looked at what had been done and said to myself, we have finally made it. However, by the time the puke was hosed away, broken mirrors replaced and our entertainers paid, we were just trading dollars. Fate was to get us out of the bar business. Like many of the colored folks, I had visions of winning big from playing the numbers. I, like others, played with the bookies. Unfortunately, the bookie that I selected was under investigation by the F.B.I and his phone lines were being monitored. Once again, the Bolden curse came into play. My voice was heard on his phone and I, along with him and his organization, were indicted. Suddenly, my whole life changed. I didn't want my reputation as a police officer to be smudged so I retired from the force. Not ever having been in trouble, I was truly worried as to what was going to happen to me.

I couldn't eat or sleep and I lost 89 pounds. My offense was so minor to have had such terrible consequences. I was sent to jail and ultimately, my dearest friend of almost 50 years and my attorney, Thomas Jacobs, had the matter expunged. The worse was yet to come. I no longer wanted any part of the bar business. Joy had to take over, which turned out badly. She became involved in a serious automobile accident coming home from the bar. After that, I put the bar up for sale. One day, while eating at Kenny Kings, I ran into a fellow, whom I had known from the neighborhood of the flower shop and was also a member of Columbia Road Baptist Church, which I had joined some years ago but no longer attended services. He began to talk to me about Jesus Christ and what he could do for me.

This was on a Monday. On Wednesday, I found myself at Columbia Road Baptist Church. It now had a new pastor, Alan

Jenkins. He was glad to see me and immediately restored me to being the announcer for the church.

Another adversity was to come into my life. My wife was stricken by a heart attack. She went through two open-heart surgeries. The first surgery was considered a success, but did not vastly improve her condition. Several months later, she was once again admitted to the hospital and underwent a second operation. Prior to the operation, all of the family had gathered at the hospital. As the gurney, on which she was being rolled to the operating room, neared me, the nurse stopped it. Joy's last words to me were "Take care of the children." It was like she knew she was not going to make it.

On Friday June 26, 1987, my beautiful Joy died during open-heart surgery. As I looked upon the tombstones of my parents, mother 1905-1995 and daddy 1906-1996, I could not help but think of the dashes between their births and deaths and all that was accomplished during their lives. If Joy had a tombstone, the dash between 1938-1987 would have represented an un-ending story of the love of a mother, the loyalty of a friend and the devotion of a wife.

After Joy's death, all I wanted was to have all of my children around me. I felt so unbelievably alone. There were so many things I had wanted to say to my wife.

Although, I still had a young teenager to raise, I considered suicide many times.

Over the years since she has gone to be with the Lord, I have re-lived every good time we ever had, as well as those periods of turmoil.

I realize regrets are of no value, but I deeply regret and have not been able to forgive myself for the times I stole from our marriage and our family.

My life, in a physical sense continued, but other than church and the day-to-day requirements of caring for my son, Freddy, I was lost in time as if cast in a void of nothingness.

Life without my wife and the stigma of having gone through a criminal process was exacting and took a tremendous toll on my life.

After my legal problems were resolved, I began to lean heavily on the Lord. He became my crutch. For many years now, I have been blessed to teach a Sunday school class of seniors.

During the years since my return to Christian fellowship, I have seen many loved ones go to be with the Lord. Although, currently a cancer patient, God gives me the necessary strength to minister to the needs of a wonderful assembly of his people. In addition to my church activities, I taught at Wooster Business College and was active in every aspect of my son's life.

My family's first holiday, after Joy went to be with the Lord, was Labor Day, 1987. My daughters and their families, gathered at our campgrounds. None of us had our hearts in it but everyone was making an effort to appear to be happy and having fun.

On May 15, 1989, I completed the academic requirements for my doctorate in Industrial psychology. So as to save money and time, I incorporated my on-campus work at Cleveland State University with distance courses from Pacific Western University in Bellaire California. I became a part of the June Graduation class. My son and I traveled to California for diploma presentation and photographs.

My wife left me with much more than memories of years gone by. She left behind a love that was so strong that my children became a part of me, just as they had been a part of her.

Fred E. Bolden, Ph.D

The most significant remembrances of my wife come by way of my children. I hear her laughter and see her motherly abilities in Rebecca. Although, Rebecca's marriage to Steven Rami, a young man with whom she had gone to school with, did not turn- out well, they

Family Photo 2002

produced four beautiful children, Rebecca and Elizabeth, who are twins and Matthew and Anthony. Beck's marriage ended in divorce and she has since remarried to Richard (Rick) Beehler. When I look at Karen, I see my wife's combatant nature and ability to survive. I never gave Karen much of a chance with her choice of beaus. She ultimately met and married Phillip Harris, an African American.

I was very disappointed in her choice and never let her or my wife forget it. I am happy that I finally came to realize that beneath his black skin beat the heart of a gentlemen and a kind soul. As the years passed, I grew to love, appreciate and respect Phillip. Their relationship has outlasted all of my other daughters' marriages. They are the proud parents of Erin Marie, a college student, Jami, a college student and Hannah Beth. Although, my daughter, Karen and I have had an estranged relationship over the years, I could not love her more. Each of us must determine within our own hearts how we will perceive others and by what measure we determine our love.

When it comes to telling someone off, my daughter, Leatrice inherited that part of her mother's character. Leatrice Joy married Daniel Linnean, a wonderful father, since divorced and is the mother of Joshua Daniel now a college student, Aaron Michael and Jacob. All fine boys and young men. Then there's my Sherry, the peacemaker and musher, just like her mother. Sherry married Victor Thomas Smith, an African-American shoe salesman and career Airmen. This relationship and ultimate marriage did not set well with me, but it took place anyway. From that marriage issued one son, Victor Thomas, a fine young man, who is currently seeking his way.

Sherry, ultimately divorced Victor and eventually met and married a contractor named Michael Schoolcraft, who was given to drink. Mike later reformed, came to know the Lord and became a wonderful husband and father to Leatrice Joy and Solomon Ray. Michael now rests with the Lord.

To our son, she left a hot temper and a strong body. He has since met and married Melissa Allen, a wonderful girl with great insight and prudence. Fred is now the father of Ethan Fredrik and Madison Joy.

He received his under- graduate and post-graduate from John Carroll University. During his high school years and most of his college years, he played football and wrestled. I attended every match and game. My beloved wife, Joy would have been so proud of him.

Many years have passed since the death of my wife, but her memories linger on and will for as long as I live be a part of my life. I rejoice that I will someday be with her and my firstborn, Allen and all those loved ones, who now rest with the Lord in heaven.

The End

About the Author

Dr. Bolden was born December 27, 1931 in Fort Worth, Texas. His family migrated to Cleveland, Ohio from Fort Worth when he was 11 years old. He was educated in Ohio and California. He attended Cleveland State University and Pacific Western University in California, where he received his Doctorate in Industrial Psychology. He spent 25 years with the Cleveland Police Department investigating accidents and teaching in the Police Academy. Upon retirement, he taught at the then Wooster Business College and later became its Dean of Student Affairs. He also taught at various proprietary colleges and guest lectured at Akron University, in addition to examining Criminal Justice programs at various universities for the Accrediting Council for Independent Colleges and Schools out of Washington D.C. He authored Several textbooks including College Skills, Help Mate (a career development book) and Training Techniques. His Doctoral Thesis was on "The correlation between knowledge, skills and ability in law enforcement". He is currently the Director of Human Resources for a Cleveland firm.

Printed in the United States
918700002B